Contents

Introduction

When was the last time you got active? What did it feel like? Even if you think it's been a while, you've probably been moving muscles without even realising it.

Time for action

Every time you move and exert yourself, you're helping to keep your body in good shape. Our bodies are like cars or machines – they need to be moved regularly to keep in top condition. Some people are more active than others. They may be fitter or more naturally able. But whatever your ability, now is the time to take action for a new, more mobile you.

Why exercise?

Apart from the fact that getting active is good for your body – helping your heart and lungs to work more efficiently, and increasing your strength and flexibility – there are other benefits

Exercising can be a great way to spend time with friends and family.

to enjoy. Exercise makes you look and feel good. It will tone and strengthen your muscles, improving your body shape and your posture.

DiD YOU KNOW?

Exercise can improve your mood. Regular activity increases the amount of endorphins (the hormones that make us feel happy) and unlocks natural antidepressants, such as serotonin, in the brain.

If you want to lose weight, regular exercise will help you to achieve your goals. It will also help to cleanse your skin and will give you a glowing vitality.

If you're prone to coughs and colds, exercise may be the answer. Regular exercise helps to boost the immune system to keep common ailments at bay. Getting active is a great way to de-stress and rest your mind, and to relax tensed muscles. It's even been shown to help improve memory and brain function! And the benefits are long-lasting. Studies have shown that regular exercise when you're young helps to reduce the risk of serious diseases in later life, such as heart disease, cancer and diabetes.

How do I go about it?

Exercise is easy to do and doesn't have to cost money or take a lot of time. While some people like to get involved in activities such as team sports, time at the gym or a jogging club, you probably already enjoy many things that keep you fit. Going for a brisk walk or swim, cycling to visit friends or helping with physical jobs around the house or garden are all good ways to get active.

After a hard day you may feel like sitting in front of the television, but exercise can give your energy levels a boost.

FEEL-GOOD FACTOR

Exercise is meant to be fun! Use it to spend time with family and friends, or as time on your own if you need a break from things. Your body will benefit, but it's a great way to enjoy yourself at the same time.

If you haven't exercised for a while, don't worry. Start gradually and over time you'll find your level of fitness increasing so you can push yourself harder. You don't have to train like a top athlete to enjoy the benefits of improved fitness. Any activity that gets you on the move – even for just a few minutes each day – is better than none at all.

More important than ever

In recent years, our world has become less physically demanding. We use cars and buses to get around, improved technology has made our work easier, and entertainment has become less active. You may think exercise is tiring – if you're feeling lethargic, surely relaxing in front of the television is what your body needs? But did you know that exercise actually helps you unlock stores of energy in your body? By giving your body a workout, you'll feel more active and ready for the challenges that each day brings.

On the Move!

To get the best from our bodies, we need to do both aerobic and anaerobic exercise. Aerobic exercise helps to increase fitness, while anaerobic exercise strengthens muscles.

Aerobic exercise

Aerobic exercise includes the activities that make you feel puffed and out of breath. They get your heart and lungs working hard to supply your muscles with oxygen (aerobic means 'with oxygen'). When you start to run or jog, for example, the muscles in your arms and legs tell your brain that they need more oxygen to produce the energy to move. You begin to breathe faster and more deeply, and your heart rate increases.

Skipping is an aerobic exercise that increases your heart rate and strengthens your heart and lungs.

As you breathe in more air, your lungs transfer the oxygen to your blood and your beating heart pumps this oxygen-rich blood around your body. This helps your muscles to work at their full potential. As a strong muscle itself, your heart also needs more oxygen to help it beat faster. Your muscles use the oxygen to break down glucose in your food to release energy.

FEEL-GOOD FACTOR

The World Health Organization recommends that teenagers do 60 minutes of moderate to vigorous activity every day for optimum health. Use this as a fitness goal to work towards!

Fighting fit

The term 'fitness' describes how much a person can do with their body. Aerobic exercise helps to improve fitness because it strengthens the heart and lungs. As these organs become stronger, they begin to use oxygen more efficiently (see pages 10–13). A strong heart and lungs means your body uses less energy to pump more oxygen to your body's cells. So the more you exercise, the easier you'll find it to stay active without getting tired.

Increased metabolism

Combining exercise with a varied diet is also a good way to maintain a healthy weight. When aerobic exercise increases the amount of oxygen in your blood, it helps to burn more energy (calories). This means that fewer unused calories are turned to fat. When you work even harder, your body begins to burn fat as well.

Your body is constantly burning energy to keep going – whether you are active or at rest. These chemical reactions, called your metabolism, help your body to stay fit and healthy. Some people have a naturally fast metabolism, but a combination of aerobic and anaerobic exercise can help to raise your metabolic rate.

Muscles burn more calories to maintain themselves than any other tissue in the body. Someone who has a more muscular body through regular exercise, for example, will burn more calories even when they are resting. A higher metabolic rate is good for maintaining a healthy weight, but it also helps release energy, giving you extra vitality.

It's only natural

Exercise is something that our bodies are designed to do. Did you know that it's easier to walk for 30 minutes than to stand still for

30 minutes? Studies have also shown that the exercising habits of our ancestors helped to influence the body's development. Our ancestors used running as a survival technique – as hunters and gatherers, they would look for vultures circling above a carcass, and run long distances to reach it before other scavengers got there.

When you exercise, your body burns the energy from the food you eat.

The aerobic system

Your heart, lungs and blood are called your aerobic system. Together, they use oxygen from the air you breathe to help unlock the energy your body needs to get active. Your heart is the strongest muscle in your body. It constantly beats but never gets tired. Your heart pumps oxygen-rich blood to your body's cells. When you exercise, your muscles need even more oxygen, so your heart has to work harder.

Heart to heart

Your heart is just behind the breastbone, slightly to the left of the middle of your chest. It has four chambers – two ventricles and two atria. When your heart beats, the atria contract and push blood into the ventricles. When the ventricles contract, blood is pushed out of the heart. The muscles then relax, and the heart chambers fill with blood again.

The right side of the heart pumps blood to the lungs to pick up oxygen (see page 12). The left side pumps oxygen-rich blood around the body. This blood travels to the cells, tissues and organs through a network of blood vessels called arteries. Your cells use the oxygen in your blood to release energy from the food you eat. At the same time, they replace the oxygen with carbon dioxide – a waste product of this process. The blood then travels back to the heart through a network of veins.

DiD YOU KNOW?

When you're resting, your heart pumps about 5 litres of blood around your body every minute. When you exercise, this can increase to about 25 litres a minute.

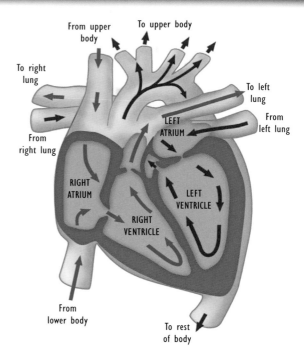

Your heart is a hard-working organ – blood travels through it more than 1,000 times a day.

Body processes

A strong heart can help other body processes, too. When your heart works efficiently, the blood flow helps to maintain a healthy body temperature. Poor blood circulation, for example, can cause the hands and feet to get cold very easily. As we get older, regular exercise can also help to prevent a narrowing or loss of small blood vessels around the body.

When you exercise, you get hot because your body is burning energy. Your skin also feels flushed. This is because your blood vessels widen to carry blood to the skin's surface, to let the heat escape. This widening of the blood vessels is good for your health. When blood flows more freely through the arteries, fatty deposits and blood clots are less likely to build up and cause illnesses such as heart disease. A widening of the arteries can also prevent, delay or reduce the symptoms of high blood pressure.

FEEL-GOOD FACTOR

There are many ways to get active. Try cycling, running, brisk walking or a group activity. Taking the stairs instead of the escalator and running for the bus are a good start! Build up your fitness gradually and soon you'll be on the road to a new, improved you.

Target zone

To get the most out of aerobic activity you need to feel puffed out. This means doing exercises that increase your heart rate to between 50 and 75 per cent of your maximum heart rate (your maximum heart rate is 220 beats per minute, minus your age). This range is called your 'target zone' (see page 26).

If you haven't exercised for a while, aim for the lower part of this range for the first few months. Start with a brisk walk or jog for just

You get flushed during exercise because your blood vessels widen to carry blood to the surface of your skin.

5, 10 or 15 minutes. Over time, you'll find that you can gradually work harder to raise your heart rate. It's important to exercise at a pace that's right for you. You should be able to talk while you work out. If you can't, you are exercising too hard – slow down and let your body recover.

If you haven't exercised for a while, try gentle jogging to begin with – or even a brisk walk!

On the Move!

Take a deep breath

Your lungs are the key to the oxygen that keeps your body going. When you breathe in, your lungs help to transfer oxygen from the air to your bloodstream. When you exercise, you breathe even more deeply to supply the extra oxygen that your body needs. The amount of air your lungs can hold is called your lung capacity. The average human can hold about six litres of air in their lungs, but only a small amount of this is used when you breathe.

The amount of air that you breathe in depends on your activity. When you're resting, you take about 15 breaths a minute (taking in about 12 litres of air). From this, your lungs absorb about 200 ml of oxygen. Most people double their air intake when they exercise. When some top athletes exercise, however, they breathe in up to 12 times as much air. This increases their breathing rate to 150 litres of air (about five litres of oxygen) a minute.

Gas exchange

Every time you take a breath, the air travels down a series of tubes from your windpipe into your lungs. The tubes divide into smaller branches called bronchi until they become tiny air sacs called alveoli. The alveoli are covered with small blood vessels called capillaries. With each breath, the alveoli fill with air and the capillaries absorb the oxygen into your blood. This oxygen-rich blood travels to your heart and is then transferred to the rest of your body to be used by your cells.

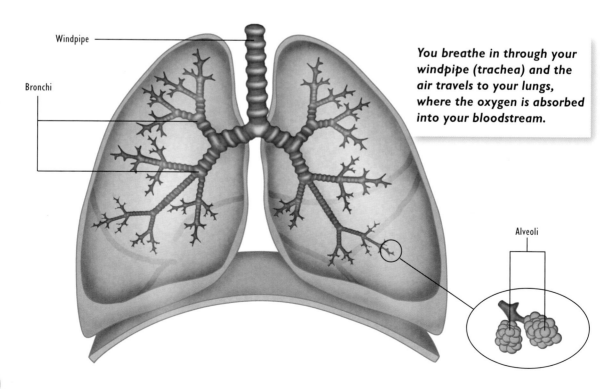

Windpipe

Bronchi

Alveoli

You breathe in through your windpipe (trachea) and the air travels to your lungs, where the oxygen is absorbed into your bloodstream.

LUNG CAPACITY

Olympic swimming champion Michael Phelps has a lung capacity thought to be double that of most humans (12 litres rather than 6 litres). His heart pumps 30 litres of oxygen-rich blood through his body every minute, aiding his record-breaking speed, strength and stamina.

The right side of the heart pumps oxygen-poor blood to the lungs – to pick up oxygen and to release carbon dioxide (see page 10). Oxygen-rich blood then returns to the left side of the heart, where it is pumped to the rest of the body. This is why the air you breathe in is rich in oxygen, while the air you breathe out is rich in carbon dioxide.

Strengthening your lungs

Regular exercise will help to strengthen the muscles in your chest and increase your lung capacity. Your lungs won't actually change in size, but they'll become more flexible and able to take in more air. They'll also become better at extracting oxygen from the air you breathe and expelling carbon dioxide. This means you'll be less likely to get out of breath when you exercise. Strong lungs reduce the strain on your heart, too, giving your heart less work to do to supply your muscles with oxygen. Try to breathe deeply when you exercise to strengthen your heart and lungs.

A peak flow meter monitors lung capacity by measuring the rate at which air is expelled from your lungs.

Build Your Strength

Anaerobic exercise involves short bursts of intense activity followed by periods of rest. Examples include sprinting or weight-lifting. Anaerobic exercise helps to strengthen your muscles.

Energy supply

While aerobic exercise gets more oxygen into your bloodstream, during anaerobic exercise your body uses up oxygen faster than your lungs can supply it (anaerobic means 'without [or with little] oxygen'). Anaerobic exercise helps you to build stronger, more flexible muscles (see pages 16–17) and improves stamina.

In aerobic exercise, your heart and lungs work hard to get oxygen to your muscles to release energy. This process can take a couple of minutes to get working. In contrast, in anaerobic exercise, your muscles need to access quick bursts of energy straight away. If there is not enough oxygen to do this, the body uses chemical sources of fuel or stored glucose in the body. Your body can only perform without oxygen for a limited time. This is why you should alternate short bursts of anaerobic activity with periods of rest.

Lifting weights is an anaerobic activity that improves stamina and muscle flexibility.

Anaerobic exercise helps to improve your general fitness, but in particular your speed and stamina. This will enable you to inject bursts of energy into your activities. If you want to be able to sprint for the bus or make that rugby try, anaerobic training will help you reach your goals.

Lactic acid

When you exercise, your muscles produce a substance called lactate. When you exercise hard, by sprinting for example, the levels of lactate increase. Sometimes, it can be difficult for your body to remove the lactate quickly from your muscles. If the lactate levels get too high, a reaction with other chemicals in the body can cause lactic acid to build up in the muscles. This is what makes your muscles feel tired or tender when you overwork.

DiD YOU KNOW?

Anaerobic exercise doesn't burn fat (your body needs oxygen to do that). However, by strengthening muscles, it speeds up your metabolic rate so you continue to burn fat after you exercise.

In small doses, lactic acid doesn't damage your body. In fact, the pain is useful because it tells you to stop working your body too hard. As you slow down, your body is able to recover and increase oxygen levels again to flush away the lactic acid. Too much lactic acid can be harmful, however. Giving your body a chance to recover between exercises helps to reduce the levels of lactic acid in your bloodstream.

A quick sprint to catch the bus gives you a burst of anaerobic activity!

Regular aerobic and anaerobic exercise can actually help your body become more efficient at removing lactic acid from your muscles. If you strengthen and build your muscles, and increase oxygen levels through improved lung capacity, your body will be able to cope with higher levels of lactic acid.

Interval training

Interval training is a particularly good way to enjoy an anaerobic workout. By alternating anaerobic exercises (short sprints or lifting weights) with periods of rest or aerobic activity, you allow your body to recover before pushing it hard again. If you already have a basic level of fitness, try walking for a minute, jogging or sprinting for 10 seconds, and then walking for a minute again. Repeating this process will help train your body to access stored energy in short, sharp bursts. Increasing your muscle strength and endurance will also help you to make muscle movements more quickly.

REAL LIFE

'I love playing in the football team, but by half-time I'm really puffed out. In the second half, it can be difficult to find the energy to sprint for the ball. My sports teacher recommended interval training, to improve my fitness and to build my speed.' Matt (14)

Build Your Strength

Body conditioning

As well as helping to condition your heart and lungs, exercise is good for muscles and bones. Exercise helps to build, maintain and strengthen bones, joints and muscles, reducing the risk of breaks and strains. A good workout also increases the flexibility and range of movement in the joints.

Muscle power

You have over 600 skeletal muscles in your body, which move and support your bones or help with delicate movements such as blinking. Some skeletal muscles are attached to your bone joints, by a flexible cord or sheet called a tendon. These skeletal muscles contract and relax to help your bones move. When two bones meet at a joint, tissues called ligaments fasten the bones together, stabilising the joint.

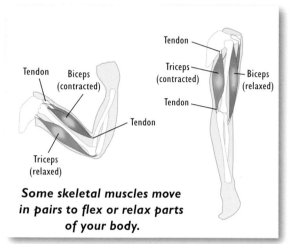

Some skeletal muscles move in pairs to flex or relax parts of your body.

Tendon Biceps (contracted)

Tendon

Tendon

Triceps (relaxed)

Tendon

Triceps (contracted)

Biceps (relaxed)

Tendon

Skeletal muscles are made of bundles of long, thin fibres called myocytes that overlap when a muscle contracts, and stretch out when a muscle relaxes. These muscle fibres contain filaments (strands) of actin or myosin proteins. Thick myosin fibres give you strength in short bursts – if you need to lift a heavy weight, for example. These fibres are sometimes called 'fast twitch' fibres. They are good for anaerobic exercise, when you need a sudden burst of strength or speed. Thinner actin fibres (or 'slow twitch' fibres) are good for aerobic exercise, when you need to work for a longer period of time. They use oxygen in your blood to release energy. These are the fibres you use if you want to run a marathon, or cycle or swim long distances.

Press-ups strengthen the muscles in the chest and shoulders.

Scientists think that humans genetically have more of one type of muscle fibre than another. Studies have shown that Olympic sprinters have about 80 per cent fast twitch fibres, while marathon runners have about 80 per cent slow twitch fibres. Muscle fibres can be enlarged with training, but genetic factors seem to affect their distribution.

Keep in shape

Your muscles need to be exercised regularly to keep them firm and strong. People who are hospitalised for a long period of time, or are confined to bed rest, find that their muscles weaken through lack of use. Weak muscles can affect your appearance – without exercise, muscles begin to shrink, changing your body's shape. Weak muscles can affect your posture because there is less support for your skeleton and joints. Weak stomach muscles can also change the position of the organs inside your body.

Building muscles

To grow and strengthen your muscles, you need to do some form of resistance (or strength) training. This means working your muscles hard for a short period of time. Anaerobic exercise helps to increase the number of filaments in your muscle fibres – the fibres literally grow to cope with the extra demands placed on them. During anaerobic exercise, the fast twitch fibres grow faster and larger than the slow twitch fibres, giving you stronger, denser muscles. Because these muscle fibres burn a lot of energy, they will also help your body to burn fat. Muscles store energy in the form of glucose, too. This means that larger, stronger muscles increase your ability to store energy.

You can strengthen almost any muscle group in the body by doing different exercises. Press-ups are a simple way to strengthen your chest, arm and shoulder muscles, for example. You can work other muscle groups using light weights. Do a few repetitive movements followed by a period of rest. In a matter of weeks, you can begin to increase the amount of weight you are lifting as you get stronger. Some sports are particularly good for building muscles. Horse riding strengthens the muscles in your legs, buttocks and back, for example.

Canoeing or kayaking trains your upper arm and back muscles, and rowing uses your back and leg muscles.

Your body uses 300 muscles to balance when standing still. Weak muscles can cause bad standing balance and poor posture, so it is important to keep your muscles strong and toned.

Build Your Strength

Keeping strong

Like muscles, your bones have a 'use it or lose it' quality. Just as muscles grow and strengthen when you place demands on them, bones become stronger and denser when they are used. You probably think your bones are like the skeletons you see in a museum, but they are actually living tissues that constantly grow and repair themselves. Like muscles, your bones respond to the stresses and strains of everyday life.

Studies have shown that on average, astronauts in space lose two per cent of their bone mass a month (whereas people usually lose two per cent a decade after the age of 35). The lack of gravity in space means that bones don't have to support the body for movement or posture. Without everyday stresses and strains, the skeleton begins to shrink. Most astronauts experience bone loss in the lower half of their bodies – the weight-bearing leg bones, for example, that are no longer used. Astronauts now use special equipment in space, with springs, elastic and vacuum pumps, to keep up their resistance training and prevent muscle wastage.

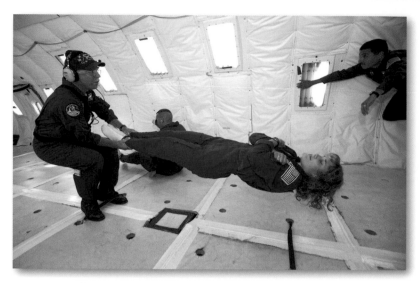

Astronauts have to train hard to keep up their muscle strength in zero-gravity conditions.

GOOD VIBRATIONS

Scientists have found that it is not just large stresses or strains on your bones that keep them growing. Small muscle twitches during everyday activities such as standing or walking have been found to affect bones. To keep your body upright, groups of muscle cells rapidly twitch. This is the slight trembling you can feel if you squat and rest your hands on your thighs.

Growing bones

When you exercise, you're telling your bone-building cells to get working. Weight-bearing exercises (when your bones and muscles work against gravity) are particularly good for your skeleton. These include aerobics, dancing, walking, jogging, climbing stairs and lifting weights. Activities that put your bones under the stress of movement and the pull of your muscles, encourage them to build more cells and become stronger. Improving and maintaining the density of your bones can also prevent serious diseases in later life such as osteoporosis, which causes the bones to weaken and break more easily.

This is especially important when you're a teenager because your bones and joints are still growing. Most bone growth happens between 10 and 16 years of age, with bone mass reaching a peak between the ages of 20 and 30. In adolescence, regular exercise can increase bone density by as much as 2–8 per cent a year. Studies have also shown that exercise as a teenager can improve bone density in later life. Women, for example, usually gain 40–50 per cent of their bone mass during adolescence. Scientists have found that women who exercised regularly during those years had a higher hip-bone density in later life than those who did not.

Keeping flexible

Your bones are too strong to bend, but your joints, and the muscles attached to them, allow them to move. Just like the oiled parts of a car, you need to move your joints regularly to keep them flexible. Exercise can actually help to strengthen your joints, too. When you build and tone your muscles, the joints that they support become stronger and firmer. This reduces the risk of injury and, by giving you good posture, helps to avoid problems of joint or back pain in later life.

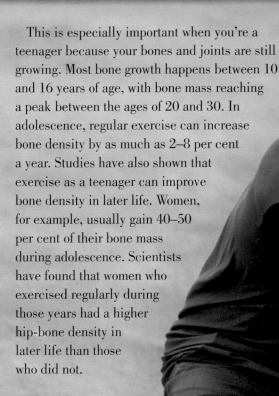

DiD YOU KNOW?

Some professional tennis players have 35 per cent more bone in their playing arm. Scientists believe this bone growth is caused by signals sent out by contracting muscles.

Brain Power

As well as giving your body a good workout, exercise is also beneficial to your brain. Studies have shown that physical activity can even build brain cells and improve your memory.

New cells

When you exercise, you increase the flow of oxygen and blood to your organs, including your brain. Studies have shown that a workout can actually improve the function of the brain, helping with school work, memory and concentration. Exercise has been found to help generate new brain cells (neurons) in the hippocampus, the area of the brain used for learning and memory. Increased oxygen and blood flow to the brain also repairs and protects existing neurons. Scientists believe that the mild stress caused by physical activity encourages these neurons to grow, in a process called neurogenesis.

Studies have shown that the memory-enhancing effects of exercise are most obvious in ageing brains, where there is room for

Keeping active through life can help the part of your brain that controls memory.

improvement and the changes are clearly seen. Exercise is thought to be particularly beneficial for patients with diseases such as Alzheimer's and Parkinson's, which are caused by a loss of neurons. People in the early stages of Alzheimer's disease have more brain volume in areas that are important to memory when they are physically fit, compared to patients who are less active.

REAL LIFE

'My gran had Alzheimer's before she died. She got confused easily and I know it frustrated her greatly. I hope I don't have the same disease when I grow old. If exercise helps, it's got to be a good thing.' Susan (14)

A look inside

Scientists were unsure exactly why exercise caused neurogenesis, but in 2008, a study at the University of North Carolina, USA, found that people who had been exercising regularly for a long period of time had more small blood vessels in their brains and more blood flow than people who were inactive. The growth of new blood vessels – angiogenesis – occurs around the body in response to regular exercise, and this new study showed that the brain is no exception. At the moment, increased brainpower has been linked to aerobic activity, but in the future new studies will look at the effect of anaerobic exercise on brain function, too.

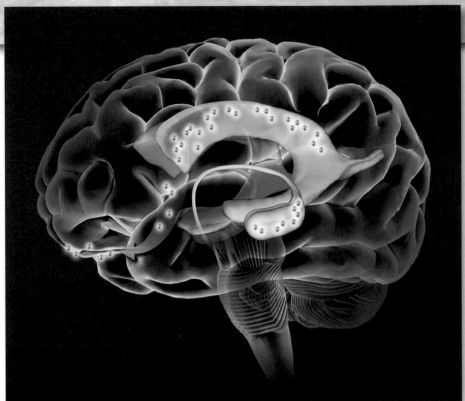

Neurogenesis is the development of new brain cells (neurons). Here, neurons develop in one part of the brain then travel to another, where they become sensory neurons.

A head start

Although studies of neurogenesis have focused on elderly patients, establishing an exercise routine in your teens is a good way to help maintain brain function in later life. At about 30 years of age, the brain starts to lose nerve tissue. Although it was once thought that brainpower diminished as cells died with age, this new research showed that the brain can continue to generate new brain cells as you get older. Aerobic activity helps to reinforce the neuron connections in your brain as you age, so that you can continue to process and store information. Don't overdo exercise on account of your brain, however. Unfortunately, it's not possible to exercise to pure brilliance!

GIVE IT A GO!

Between 6 and 15 years of age, the human brain grows most in the parietal lobes, which affect movement and physical coordination, and the temporal lobes, which affect language abilities. The skills you learn as a child and teenager are 'hardwired' in the brain. If you want to learn a new sport, now is the time to try out new skills!

Brain Power

Exercise releases endorphins in your brain – these are the chemicals that make you feel happy!

REAL LIFE

'It was exam time and I was feeling really stressed. Mum said I should go out and get some fresh air, but I had too much work to do. Then Chris called and suggested football in the park. Just an hour's game really helped to clear my head, and I had the best night's sleep in ages.'
David (15)

Happy times

While we may not be able to exercise to intellectual heights, there are no limits to the ways that exercise can make us feel good. Vigorous exercise, such as swimming, running or cycling, helps to release endorphins that encourage feelings of happiness. These hormones are usually released by the pituitary gland in the brain in response to stress or pain. They help to minimise any aches and pains that you might feel when you exercise and can produce a feeling of euphoria. Endorphins usually start to take effect after about 30 minutes of physical activity.

For people who exercise vigorously on a regular basis, the release of endorphins can have an addictive effect – the more you exercise, the more you need to do to achieve the same level of euphoria. But unlike some addictions – such as drink or drugs – the 30-minute delay in endorphin release means that few people get truly addicted to exercise. It's important, however, not to allow exercise to become an obsession.

Relieving depression

Exercise can also help relieve symptoms of depression and anxiety. Studies have shown that people who are physically active recover more quickly from bouts of mild depression.

The increased blood flow caused by exercise can help to flush away waste products from the brain that build up when you're stressed or working hard.

Regular exercise can also protect mental health as we age, because it increases levels of natural antidepressants in the brain, such as serotonin and norepinephrine. Scientists have also found that depression can be alleviated by neurogenesis (see page 20). In depressed women, for example, the brain's hippocampus has been found to be up to 15 per cent smaller than usual.

Relaxing your mind

Whatever the brain-boosting benefits of exercise, it's certain that a workout in the fresh air will help to relax and ease your mind. This is especially important if you're working your brain extra hard – with exams or coursework, for example. By improving blood flow to the brain, exercise brings more oxygen and nutrients that help you to think clearly. By helping to release endorphins into the bloodstream, exercise can make you feel more positive and better able to cope with stressful situations. It will also help you to get a good night's rest – a healthy body, with tired muscles, finds it easier to relax and sleep.

FEEL-GOOD FACTOR

A relaxed mind is good for your circulatory system. Stress and tension can cause your blood vessels to deteriorate as you get older and can raise your blood pressure. Taking action to keep stress levels down is a sure way to a healthier you.

Improving Fitness

Regular exercise affects how well your heart, lungs, muscles and brain work, but it also affects how long you can keep going (your stamina) and how flexible your body is (your suppleness).

Olympic marathon runners like Samuel Kamau Wanjiru train for years to build up their stamina for the long race.

Increased stamina

When you exercise, your body uses energy to keep itself going. If you have stamina, you can run a long way without getting puffed out. Stamina isn't something that you either have or don't have. It's something you can work at to build up gradually.

To improve your stamina, you need to train your body to become more efficient, so it uses less energy when you move around. The best way to improve your stamina is to strengthen your heart and lungs through aerobic activity. Making your heart work harder can thicken the heart muscle, giving it more power to push out blood. A strong heart can squirt out more blood with each heartbeat, so it can beat less while you do the same

FEEL-GOOD FACTOR

Skipping is one of the most effective exercises for boosting levels of stamina. Believe it or not, 10 minutes of skipping requires about the same effort as a 30-minute run. You could even learn new tricks with a skipping rope to liven up your stamina training.

amount of exercise with less effort. In the same way, if you increase your lung capacity (see page 12), your body can absorb more oxygen with fewer breaths. The more exercise you do, the easier it gets.

How much is enough?

You need to get puffed when you do aerobic exercise to really improve your fitness. During aerobic exercise, your pulse rate should rise slightly for a sustained period of time (see page 26). Short bursts of intense exercise that make your pulse rate rocket won't be effective for your overall fitness – you'll just feel exhausted and will need to stop.

There are some great physical activities out there to help you to develop stamina – rowing, canoeing, dancing, windsurfing, volleyball,

Aerobic sports such as basketball are great for increasing your stamina and making your body use energy more efficiently.

football, basketball or even housework are just a few examples. Find an activity that you enjoy and build up gradually. Keep an exercise diary of how you find each session. You'll be amazed at how much progress you make in just a few weeks.

Muscle strength

Strengthening and toning your muscles through anaerobic exercise will also help your body to endure sudden bursts of energy and will give you added strength for everyday tasks. As you increase the muscle fibres in your body, your muscles will store extra energy for when you need it most (see page 17). You'll also train your body to effectively access this stored energy for times when the oxygen supply to your muscles is limited.

REAL LIFE

'I've never been the sporty one in the class. If you said to me last year I'd be a regular runner, I'd have laughed! But I gave it go – just one length of the park at first, and now I'm running for an hour, three times a week. It's a great feeling to be able to just keep going.'
Lizzie (16)

Improving Fitness

You can feel your pulse in your wrist.

Measuring fitness

When you exercise, your heart beats faster. This means that your pulse rate increases, too. The pulse can be felt in places of the body where an artery can be lightly compressed against a bone – in your wrist or your neck, for example. The pressure of blood flowing through the arteries causes a pulse. This is not a measure of the speed at which your blood is flowing – a pulse rate is usually about 10–15 times faster than actual blood flow. Pulse rates vary from person to person and slow down as you get older. As you become fitter, you'll also find that your pulse rate becomes lower, both at rest and when you exercise. This is because your heart has been trained to work less hard at supplying your muscles with oxygen.

Taking your pulse

Your pulse rate shows the number of times your heart beats in one minute. To take your pulse, place your index and second finger on the palm side of your wrist, below the base of your thumb. Alternatively, you can place these fingers on your neck, on one side of your windpipe. Press lightly until you feel the blood pulsing below your fingers. You may need to adjust your fingers slightly until you feel the movement. Use a watch with a second hand to count how many pulses you can feel for 10 seconds. Multiply this number by six to get your pulse rate per minute.

To find out if you are exercising in your target zone (see page 11), take a break from your activity and check your 10-second pulse. This will help you to know whether you need to increase or reduce your level of exertion.

If you become out of breath when you exercise, give your body a chance to slow down.

If you find it difficult to take your pulse when you exercise, you can also figure out how effectively you're working by how you feel. You should be slightly out of breath when you exercise, but still be able to talk. If you can't, you've pushed yourself too hard. Slow down until you get your breath back.

Keeping fit

Although your pulse rate drops as you get fitter, a low pulse rate doesn't mean you should stop exercising altogether.

RESTING HEART RATE	
Age	**Beats per minute**
Up to 1	100–160
1–10	60–140
10+	60–100
Athletes	10 60

TARGET HEART RATE DURING EXERCISE	
Age	**Beats per minute**
15	123–164
20	120–160
25	117–156
30	114–152

As your stamina increases, you'll find that you need to do more to keep your pulse rate in the target zone and for your fitness level to rise. Everyone's pulse rate is different, so get used to what works for you. And work to the level of fitness you want to achieve. Not everyone strives to be fit enough to complete a half-marathon – what's more important is that your fitness levels are helping to improve your quality of life.

Stretch and Flex

Keeping on the move is one thing, but if you're strong and supple, too, you'll find that you can do more with your body and move with greater confidence.

Suppleness

The stretchier your muscles and tendons are, the more supple you are. Suppleness helps you to move your body smoothly and confidently, without jarring. Flexible muscles are also the key to good posture and coordination. Stretching helps to tone muscles throughout your body, and your movements become less restricted as your muscles grow more flexible. More importantly, suppleness can affect the way that you move when you exercise, making you less likely to suffer from strains, sprains or stiffness. Tight or stiff muscles put pressure on your joints when you exercise and can lead to an injury.

If you're supple, you find it easy to bend, stretch and twist into different positions.

Longer muscles

Stretching is a great way to improve suppleness and flexibility. Your skeletal muscles stretch to a certain length when you move and contract them. This length is determined by the suppleness of your muscles as well as the suppleness of the tendons and ligaments that keep them in place. Stretching can gently encourage the ligaments, tendons and muscles to lengthen. It also gives room for the blood vessels to expand, helping to increase the blood flow through your body.

Limbering up

It's good to stretch before and after you exercise. Stretching after a light warm-up will improve the flexibility of your joints and muscles, and make you less likely to experience strains and sprains (see page 34). After exercise, stretching can relieve any tightness in your muscles and help the body to recover as you cool down. You'll find it easier to stretch after you've been active. This is because blood flow has increased and your body has warmed up.

Whatever type of exercise you decide to do, it is important to stretch before you begin.

By doing gentle exercises, you can gradually stretch the tissues around your muscles to make your muscles and tendons longer and stronger. But remember, everyone is different – some people have longer, looser muscles than others. You may find it difficult to touch your toes, while your friend can put their fingertips on the floor. That's okay! Don't stretch yourself beyond what feels comfortable for you.

Stretch and Flex

Take a break

Stretching can be done at any time of day, and it's a great way to relax and de-stress. Your muscles work hard throughout the day, even when you're standing or sitting still. Taking time out to stretch your muscles helps increase the blood flow around your body and gives your muscles a breather.

During your teenage years you spend a lot of time sitting in school and in front of a computer. It's difficult to remember to stretch, but there are lots of simple exercises you can do, even when sitting down. Now is the time to develop a good posture to avoid joint and back pain when you get older, and to keep your joints strong and supple.

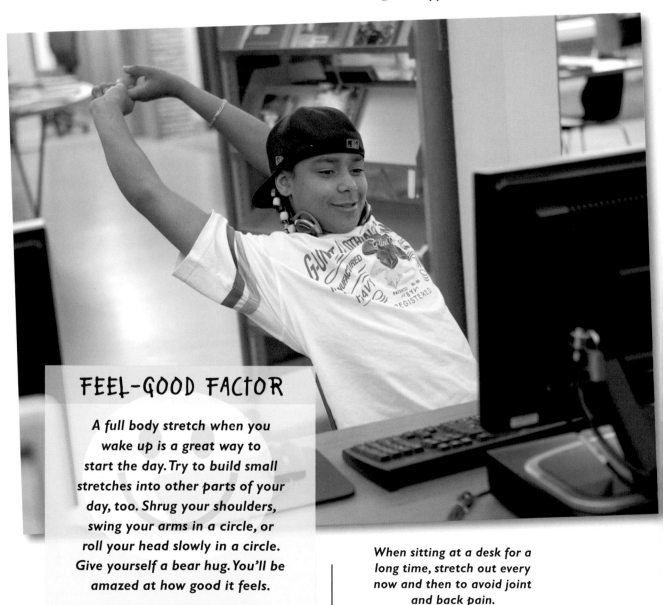

FEEL-GOOD FACTOR

A full body stretch when you wake up is a great way to start the day. Try to build small stretches into other parts of your day, too. Shrug your shoulders, swing your arms in a circle, or roll your head slowly in a circle. Give yourself a bear hug. You'll be amazed at how good it feels.

When sitting at a desk for a long time, stretch out every now and then to avoid joint and back pain.

Stretching exercises

Try these simple stretching exercises to improve your flexibility. Stretch slowly and gently, without sudden movements or jerks that could pull or strain a muscle. Don't bounce when you stretch – this can strain your muscles before they are properly warmed up. If you include gentle stretching as part of your exercise routine, in a few weeks you'll find that you're able to move and stretch more than ever before.

Front thigh muscles and buttocks

Hold on to a chair or lean your right hand against a wall. Bend your left leg up behind you and hold your left foot gently with your left hand. Hold for five seconds. Repeat three times on each side.

Front thigh muscles

Kneel on your left knee and put your right foot on the floor in front of you. With your hands on your right knee slowly raise up your left knee. Hold for five seconds. Repeat three times on each side.

Hamstring (back leg) muscles

Balance yourself and put one leg carefully on a low stool or chair. Straighten this leg. Bend the other knee gently to stretch your hamstring. Repeat three times on each side.

Bottom muscles

Lie on your back with your legs bent. Bring one knee up and gently pull it towards your chest. Hold for five seconds. Repeat three times on each side.

Stretch and Flex

Keep up your strength

How strong you are depends on the amount of force that your muscles can produce. The stronger you are, the easier you'll find it to lift or move a heavy weight for a short period of time. If you have endurance, too, you'll be able to lift or move lighter weights repeatedly for longer periods.

Building strength

To make yourself stronger, you can train particular muscles (or muscle groups) that you use in everyday life. Strengthening your leg muscles will help you to walk or run up hills or stairs. Strengthening your arm and shoulder muscles will help you to lift heavy books or shopping bags. Strengthening exercises help to increase the size of your muscle fibres (see page 17) and if you exercise regularly you'll maintain this strength for longer.

Strengthening exercises don't just benefit your muscles. As you train, you'll be strengthening your bones and the tendons that keep your joints stable. You'll improve your posture, and you'll find that your stamina increases, too.

Using weights is a good way to give an added boost to your exercise regime.

Weight training

If you want to try some anaerobic exercise to increase your muscles, lifting light weights will help to get you started. You need to do enough repetitions so your muscles feel tired. Always use a weight that feels comfortable to lift. A tin of tomatoes is often a good starting point!

REAL LIFE

'I went on the school ski trip last year. We were given exercises to help strengthen our leg muscles. It was hard work at first, but after a week or so they began to get easier. When I got back, I also found I could cycle a bit faster to Sam's house!'
Joe (16)

As you increase your strength gradually, you'll find that you can move on to slightly heavier loads. Ideally, the weight should be heavy enough for your muscles to tire in less than 12 repetitions, but light enough that you can do at least 4 repetitions. Remember to rest between repetitions and have at least one day off between working the same muscle groups, to give your muscles a chance to recover.

Where's the limit?

Don't be disheartened if you find that your progress levels out. Scientists believe that there are limits to the strength, speed or jumping height that even the top athletes can achieve. Since the first modern Olympics in 1896, athletes have been increasing their speed, year on year. In 1896, for example, the men's 100-metre gold medallist, Tom Burke, ran at a speed of 30 km/h. In 2009, Usain Bolt ran at more than 37.5 km/h!

However, scientists believe that this continued increase can't last forever. The biological functions of organs such as the lungs have limited potential. Having said that, improved sports equipment, such as running suits and shoes, improved diets and coaching techniques, may well see more records broken.

Usain Bolt has been nicknamed 'Lightning Bolt' because of his incredible speed at sprinting.

DiD YOU KNOW?

The strongest muscle in the body (based on weight) is the masseter muscle, located in the jaw. It can clench the teeth with a force of up to 25 kg on the incisors, or 91 kg on the molars.

Keeping Safe

Exercise is meant to be fun, so it's important that you keep safe when you get active to enjoy your workout as much as possible.

Warming up

One of the most important things to do before you get active is to warm up. Warming up raises your heart rate so you can start to get extra oxygen-rich blood to your muscles. As your body gets warmer, your muscles become more flexible and your joints become more mobile. Stretching and loosening your muscles, limbs and joints (see page 31) will get your body ready for action and reduce your risk of injury. You should begin exercising at a medium pace to give your body a chance to adjust to the new movements. After about five minutes, you should be warm enough to push yourself harder.

Cooling down

After you exercise, cooling down will help your body to recover and enable your breathing and heart rate to return to normal. Slow down your movements gradually until you are still – by changing from running to brisk walking, for example. If you stop straight away, you may feel dizzy. Stopping gradually also gives your body time to remove lactic acid from your muscles (see page 15).

You may have seen marathon runners wrapped in foil blankets after a race. This ensures that they don't lose their body heat too quickly.

Bend and stretch a little to relax your muscles. This will help to keep your joints supple and will prevent any symptoms of stiffness the next day. Exercise makes you hot, so take care not to cool down too quickly. Put an extra layer of clothing on when you cool down to avoid getting too chilly.

Know your limits

Listen to your body when you exercise. If you feel faint, dizzy or out of breath, it's a sign that you need to take a break! Slow down and let

your body recover. Think about how you want exercise to work for you. Perhaps your aims are to improve your aerobic stamina or to tone your muscles, or a little of both. Even top athletes can't do everything. The chances are that a marathon runner can't lift heavy weights, and a shot-putter can't run long distances. Keep your activities fun and your aims realistic.

Over-exercising, especially if you're tired, can lead to strains and sprains, or more serious injuries, so take a break if you feel you've pushed yourself too hard!

Keeping Safe

Safety first

You don't need expensive equipment to get active, but you should take care to wear suitable clothes and shoes. On cold days, try to wear layers of clothing to keep you warm. Clothes that are loose fitting (but not too baggy) will help you move around comfortably. Materials that absorb sweat, such as cotton, are better than synthetic materials that can make you feel hot. Choose well-fitting trainers that give your foot and ankle adequate support. And tie your shoelaces securely to avoid tripping over.

If you do use equipment, such as gymnastics apparatus or heavy weights, it's important to have adult supervision. Instructions and guidelines are designed to help you avoid injury. Make sure that you warm up well before you get active. If your body is cold, you'll need more energy to warm up so you'll tire more easily. Less blood travels to cold muscles, which makes them more prone to injury.

Fuel and liquids

Try not to exercise just after you've eaten. When your body is digesting, your bloodstream is busy helping your stomach break down and absorb your food. This means your muscles will have less blood flowing to them and will be unable to work at their full potential. Exercising too soon after a meal can also make you feel sick or faint. Try to avoid strenuous exercise for at least two hours after you've eaten. If you exercise first, it's better to leave about 20 minutes before having a meal.

It's important to take in fluids both during and after exercise. When you exercise you lose water as you sweat, so you need to drink more to replace it. Water is essential for your body's cells to function effectively.

Try to drink little and often during exercise, rather than all at once.

Where and when?

Exercising outdoors in the fresh air is the best way to give your body the oxygen it needs. But take care on very hot days in summer. You may prefer to exercise in the morning or the evening when the sun is less severe. If you have bad hay fever, exercise in the morning when the pollen count is lower. If you live in a city and like to jog, the morning may also be better, before smoke and fumes fill the air.

In the evening, make sure you wear light or reflective clothing when it gets dark and face oncoming traffic if you jog beside a road. Try to jog on soft ground (rather than concrete). Hard surfaces can jar and damage your joints.

FEELING FRESH

Studies have shown that exercising in the fresh air helps to increase alertness and raise your spirits. Outdoor exercise can also burn more energy, especially when it's chilly. Your body uses up to 50 per cent more calories just to keep warm. Running on uneven and unfamiliar ground also tones more muscles than an indoor surface.

Exercising outside, such as doing tai chi, increases your oxygen intake and helps keep you alert.

Aches and pains

Most injuries happen when you're tired, so learn to know when you've done enough. Try to work at improving your stamina so you get less tired when you exercise. Don't be too ambitious – you're more prone to injure yourself if you push yourself too hard. Do what feels right for you.

A good technique is also important to avoid straining or over-stretching. Work at improving your skills and your coordination before you push your body too hard. This will help reduce your risk of injury and will make your exercise routine more effective.

Strains and sprains

You can pull or tear a muscle if it contracts strongly and the opposite muscle doesn't contract quickly enough. Warming up before you exercise and keeping your body supple will help to prevent these stresses and strains. If you feel a sharp pain when you exercise, stop at once. A hot, relaxing bath can help most minor muscle strains. If a pain continues, however, seek advice from your doctor.

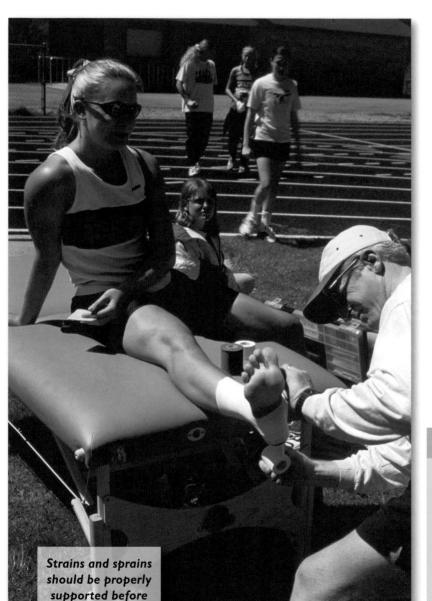

Strains and sprains should be properly supported before continuing exercise.

DiD YOU KNOW?

If you strain a muscle, you should rest it for between three and five days. During this time, your body produces chemicals and cells to help remove dead muscle fibres and begin the repair process.

Cramp

You've probably experienced cramp at some time in your life. Cramp is a sharp pain caused by a muscle (or group of muscles) going into spasm, which means they contract but don't relax again. Cramp can occur if your body is in an awkward position, or if you work your body too hard. Cramp can also be caused by a lack of nutrients and fluid in muscle fibres. Warming up properly, eating a good, balanced diet and drinking small amounts of fluid while you exercise is usually enough to avoid cramp. If you do get cramp, however, gently stretch, rub and massage the affected area to relieve the symptoms.

If you get a stitch, slow down or stop and bend forwards. Breathing deeply while pressing gently on the painful area can also help to relieve symptoms.

Stitches

A stitch is a sudden sharp pain in your side, just under your ribs. It may cause you to slow down or stop exercising altogether. Warming up and not eating too close to physical activity reduces the risk of getting a stitch. There are a number of theories about why a stitch develops. When you exercise, blood moves away from the diaphragm – the muscle that separates the stomach and abdomen from the heart and lungs. This is thought to weaken the diaphragm, causing it to cramp. Other theories point to food and fluids that are slow to digest, causing the stomach to 'tug' on the ligaments connected to the diaphragm.

Professional sportsmen and women put their muscles under great pressure when they compete.

FOOTBALL FOCUS

In a survey of injuries at a professional football club, nearly 27 per cent of all injuries involved muscles and tendons. The body's muscles and tendons have to produce large forces for sprinting, jumping, shooting and heading the ball.

Exercise for Life

To stay fit and healthy, try to make exercise a regular part of your routine. The more activity you build into your day, the better your body will feel and function.

Good timing

Find a routine that works for you. We all have busy lives and it can be difficult to find time for all the things we want to do. Choose a good time of day. Some people are more alert in the mornings and like to start their day with a burst of energy. Others prefer to wait until later in the day. Some people find that exercising in the evening relaxes their body

FEEL-GOOD FACTOR

Regular activity can help you to feel, look and work better. Exercise also helps you to learn about yourself, your abilities, your potential and your limitations. It gives you confidence in yourself and helps you to work with others. There's no doubt that getting active is the first step to enjoying a fuller life.

and helps them to sleep more deeply. Others find that exercising too close to bedtime makes it harder to fall asleep because their mind is racing.

If you often feel tired, remember that improving fitness will help your body to access more energy. Regular activity will help to reduce this fatigue and make you feel more alert each day.

Just taking the dogs for a walk is good exercise – and a good habit to get into.

A regular routine

Once you've identified the times that are best for you, try to make activities a part of your regular routine. If you get used to a weekly workout, you'll find it easier to keep up your fitness goals and exercise will feel less like a chore. Choose activities you like – that way you'll be more likely to do them regularly and enjoy the benefits that they bring. Remember that exercise can be spread over the week. Sometimes you may only manage 10–15 minutes. The important thing is to make physical activity a regular goal.

It only takes a few minutes a day to become more physically active. For a start, you could run up the stairs, or have a brisk walk to the post box. To condition your heart and lungs, up to an hour of regular exercise, three or four times a week is recommended. But if time is an issue, don't let that stop you. Try to find two 15-minute periods or even three 10-minute periods a week. Once you realise how enjoyable a workout can be, you may want to make it a habit! This way, exercise becomes a part of your life without you even realising it.

A LONGER LIFE

Scientists have discovered that a good daily workout can add four years to your life. In a US study, people who exercised moderately (such as walking for 30 minutes a day, five days a week) lived up to 1.5 years longer than those who were less active. Those who did more vigorous activity (such as running for the equivalent time) lived nearly four years longer.

Joining a club or attending a class can help to make exercise a part of your weekly routine.

Exercise for Life

Skateboarding, pilates, or just kicking a football in the park are all good ways to spend your time and get fit.

Good to be young

Studies have shown that teenagers who exercise regularly are more likely to make exercise a lifelong habit. It's never too soon to start! Exercise will improve your life now, but you will also feel the benefits in the years ahead. Regular exercise as a teenager can also reduce the risk of illnesses in later life, such as heart disease, high blood pressure, osteoporosis, obesity, arthritis and cancer.

As you get older, your body changes. Your muscles weaken, your joints become less flexible, and some of your muscle tissue is replaced by fat. Regular exercise when you're young helps you to stay fit through these changing years.

FEEL-GOOD FACTOR

You don't have to be athletic to exercise. Most physical activities can be done without special skills. Walking is a perfect example! Whatever your ability, today is the perfect time to get active for a healthier, happier life.

Keeping at it

Many teenagers stop doing organised sport as they get older. Once you leave school, physical education classes become a thing of the past and it can be difficult to branch out on your own. Unless you like jogging, or you find a group activity that doesn't cost too much, it can be difficult to know where to start. But remember all the health benefits that an active lifestyle brings.

Choose activities that are right for you. You don't have to be sporty to enjoy getting active. Perhaps you'd rather do an exercise DVD at home. You could even start by introducing physical activities into your daily routine – walking to school or your job instead of taking the bus, doing active chores such as gardening at home, or finding a part-time job that gets you on the move.

If you have specific goals in mind, a variety of activities could help to maximise the benefits of your exercise. Running will help to improve stamina, yoga or dance will aid your flexibility, and resistance training will improve your strength and give you a well-rounded workout. Set your sights on both short- and long-term goals and keep a record of your progress. It will probably inspire you to keep going! Above all, choose activities that you enjoy.

Look ahead

Look at exercise as a way to do activities with your friends or family, and an opportunity to meet new people. Next time you're faced with a challenging walk or an uphill struggle, think about what benefits the activity is having on your body, and over time, just what your body will be able to do for you.

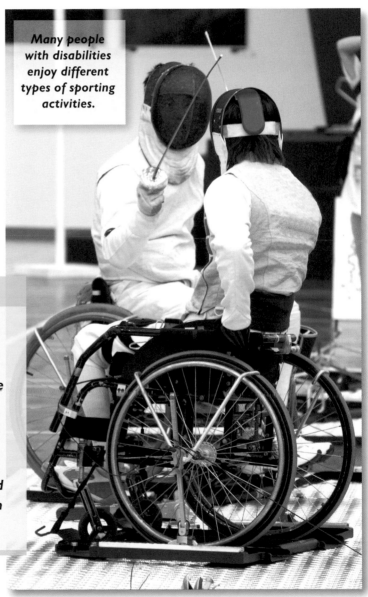

Many people with disabilities enjoy different types of sporting activities.

EXERCISE FOR ALL

If you have a disability, there may be different challenges for you, but it is still important to exercise and there are plenty of ways to get active. Some amazing athletes have disabilities. Trischa Zorn, a Paralympic swimmer, for example, competed in seven Paralympic Games. Blind since birth, she holds the record for the most gold medals (41) ever won by an athlete in the Olympics or the Paralympics.

Glossary

aerobic exercise any type of exercise that makes the heart and lungs work harder, pumping oxygen-rich blood to the muscles.

Alzheimer's disease a disease of the brain that causes dementia.

anaerobic exercise strenuous exercise that makes the muscles use energy without oxygen.

angiogenesis the formation of new blood vessels in the body.

arteries blood vessels that carry oxygen-rich blood from the heart to the cells, tissues and organs of the body.

blood pressure the force that blood exerts on the walls of the blood vessels. Blood pressure can vary according to age and general health.

blood vessel a vein, artery or capillary that carries blood around the body.

calorie a unit for measuring the amount of energy in food. One calorie is the amount of energy needed to raise the temperature of one gram of water by 1°C.

cancer a disease caused by a growth or tumour resulting from an abnormal and uncontrolled division of body cells.

diabetes an illness in which the level of glucose (sugar) in the blood is not properly controlled by the body.

diaphragm the large, flat muscle attached to the bottom of your rib cage that moves to enlarge the chest cavity so your lungs can expand when you breathe in.

endorphins hormones found mainly in the brain that reduce the sensation of pain and produce a feeling of well-being.

endurance the ability to withstand prolonged activity. Also known as stamina.

glucose a type of sugar that your body cells convert into energy.

heart disease a narrowing or blockage of the blood vessels that provide oxygen-rich blood to the heart, caused by a build-up of fatty substances in the blood vessels that restrict blood flow.

heart rate the number of heartbeats per unit of time, usually expressed as beats per minute.

hormones chemical messengers produced by glands in the body. Hormones are transported by the blood to instruct cells and organs to work in a particular way.

immune system a system of organs, tissues, cells and substances that protect the body against disease and infection.

ligaments fibrous tissues that fasten bones together across a joint.

metabolism the chemical reactions that take place in the body to maintain life and to carry out vital processes.

neurogenesis the growth and development of nervous tissue.

obesity when a person has an abnormally high amount of body fat.

osteoporosis a disease that causes the bones to weaken and makes them more prone to breaking.

Parkinson's disease a disease of the nervous system that causes tremors and slow movement.

skeletal muscles muscles that are mostly attached to bones.

suppleness how flexible your body is.

tendons the long, stringy fibrous tissues that attach muscles to bones.

veins blood vessels that carry oxygen-poor blood back to the heart.

Further Information

Books

*Ask CosmoGIRL! About Nutrition and Fitness
(Ask Cosmo Girl)*
(Hearst, 2008)

Exercise (It's Your Health)
by Beverley Goodger
(Smart Apple Media, 2005)

Fitness (Teen Issues)
by Joanna Watson and Joanna Kedge
(Raintree Publishers, 2005)

Fitness for Life: Middle School Student Textbook
by Charles B. Corbin, Guy Le Masurier and Dolly
Lambdin
(Human Kinetics Europe Ltd, 2007)

*The Best You Can Be:
A Teen's Guide to Fitness and
Nutrition (Science of Health)*
by Rae Simons
(Mason Crest Publishers, 2005)

Personal Fitness for You
by Roberta Stokes and Sandra Schultz
(Hunter Textbooks, 2006)

Websites

http://www.teenshealth.org
Information and advice about fitness and
keeping healthy.

http://www.teenissues.co.uk
Top tips for a healthy, active lifestyle.

**http://www.teensexercise.com/Exercise.
html**
Get motivated to make exercise a part of
your life.

http://www.toneteen.com
An interactive website suggesting exercises
for different parts of the body.

**http://www.growingkids.co.uk/
TeensExerciseCategory.html**
Find out about different physical activities
and how you can get involved.

http://www.kidsexercise.co.uk
Discover more about exercise and its effect
on the body.

Index

Contents

The power of persuasion

The old car parked three doors down has a piece of paper in the rear window, with hand lettering: 'For Sale 80,000 miles Long MOT Offers above £500.' Posters in the local supermarket spell out bargain prices for milk, bottled water and chicken. Everyone at school is repeating the catchphrase from a television commercial selling breakfast cereal.

The miracle of love

A girl's joy, flowering like a rose, is radiant and full in the lovely miracle of love awakening. And for her a star, blazing bright as her dreams, will recall this moment always. Her engagement diamond, fair spark of eternity, reflects the light of her happiness in changeless splendor, and treasures its tender message of love until the end of time.

Remember, color, cutting and clarity, as well as carat weight, contribute to a diamond's beauty and value. A trusted jeweler is your best adviser. Extended payments can usually be arranged.

a diamond is forever

De Beers Consolidated Mines, Ltd.

The message is king

Each of those examples is a type of advertising. And while people tend to think of advertising as being expensive and glossy – like the cereal commercial or full-page colour ads in fashion or car magazines – the term describes a wide range of approaches.

What every advertisement shares with all the others, no matter how expensive or professionally produced, is the urge to communicate. The owner or maker of something wants to let people know about it. And then, having learned about it, people will

The De Beers diamond company found its luxury products hard to sell in the tough years of the 1940s. But its slogan 'A diamond is forever' helped to turn diamonds into symbols of eternal love.

want to learn more or even buy the product or service. In other words, advertising is concerned with passing on information. Advertisers pay for the space (in a newspaper or magazine) or time (on the radio or television) to get their message across.

Most societies assume that advertising helps both manufacturers and buyers. Advertisers hope that the people at the receiving end of this information – readers, listeners or viewers – will become buyers or consumers of what they are advertising. The producers of the advertised goods and services then earn back the money they spent on advertising (and they hope much more) through increased sales. This view believes that advertising informs the public and benefits those producing things.

Advertising can be defended in other ways. For example, the fashion magazine running lavish colour ads can use some of the advertising money to produce its own glossy colour photographs of the latest fashions. Without the ad money to pay for the colour, the magazine would be forced either to run only black and white photos or to charge a lot more for each issue. Similarly, radio stations in many countries depend on advertising money to stay in business.

When things go wrong

If all this sounds too good to be true, making it seem as though advertising makes the world go round – it is. Some people are misled by advertising that fails to tell the whole truth, or even tells untruths, about something. Others find themselves uncertain about where an informative news story in a newspaper or on television changes into a thinly-veiled advertisement.

The different media that use ads have guidelines and rules which govern advertising. But in a fast-changing world, people need to be aware of the fine line that divides persuading from misleading. The best advertising is lively, amusing and ground-breaking. Consumers must be able to celebrate this while staying alert about the information they are receiving.

The language of advertising

Sellers have always tried to attract other people (customers) to try their products, whether they are stallholders yelling out the latest price of grapes, or banks running television commercials so that people will use their services. The way in which companies and individuals grab people's attention is called advertising.

The origin of the word advertising helps us understand how it works. The word comes from two Latin words – *ad*, meaning 'to', and *vertere*, meaning 'turn'. So advertising is a way of turning people's attention

towards something (the product being advertised) and away from other products that might be competitors. Just attracting people's attention can make an enormous difference, tempting them to part with their money.

Today, no company can expect to survive without advertising. And because of that, the advertising industry is enormously important. Zenith Optimedia, a London-based media specialist, estimates that companies spend about £225 billion around the world every year on advertising. This figure includes spending on all sorts of advertising – books, magazines, television, radio and the Internet.

The birth of an industry

Advertising wasn't always such a money-making industry. When it began, it could hardly be called an industry at all. Despite the Latin roots of the word advertising, the ancient Romans (like other early civilizations) did not use what we would call advertising. Stalls and shops had signs showing what was being sold, and maybe where the goods came from.

In medieval Europe, towns and cities bought what they needed from local merchants and craftsmen. Butchers sold meat, wheelwrights made and repaired wagon wheels, tailors made clothing, and so on. If there was more than one of these merchants in a town, people chose one or the other because of their reputation. As the number of people who bought these goods and services was limited (because people rarely left their village or town), there was little reason to try to attract new customers.

Opposite: bright and colourful signs cover most of the walls in the heart of Tokyo's central shopping district. Successful, eye-catching advertisements have helped Japan to become one of the world's leading trading nations.

Advertising as we know it began during the seventeenth century, as a direct result of one of the most important inventions in history – the printing press. New techniques had made it cheaper to print books and other documents. They also gave birth to newspapers, which helped to spread ideas and information across a city or a region on a regular basis. Merchants began paying for lines of text to appear in newspapers, as advertising. These early advertisements were what we now call classified advertising, which are simple descriptions of products and their prices.

New products, new techniques

The Industrial Revolution, which developed in Britain during the eighteenth century and spread to Europe and North America, changed the way things were advertised. Manufacturers began to produce more goods than local people could buy; their goods also cost less because they were mass-produced. So more people could afford to buy more things. As a result, the producers of goods began to advertise them, so new customers would buy them. Advertisements in newspapers and magazines became longer and more involved.

By the nineteenth century, advertising had become more sophisticated. For the first time, advertisers combined images with text (describing a product, and why people should buy it). Illustrated advertisements appeared as posters and were printed in newspapers and magazines. Advertising helped businesses to attract new customers and retain the loyalty of existing customers. However, companies could not afford departments to produce a wide range of advertisements. So specialist advertising companies, called agencies, developed during the late nineteenth and early twentieth century.

As well as producing advertisements for their clients, agencies spent money to find out about people's preferences and tastes. Understanding what people want – and how they would like to be told about it – became as important as informing people about a company's product. The advertising industry adapted to many changes during the

This late nineteenth century ad for a magic lantern (an early form of film projector) captures the excitement of an era when new products appeared on the market almost every day.

A PROFITABLE INVESTMENT TO ALL
A $25.00 LANTERN FOR $12.00
50% $100 PER NIGHT EASILY EARNED
THE WORLD MAGIC LANTERN
ELECTRO-RADIANT
SCIENCE & ART COMBINED
TO THE BABY AMUSING YOUTH INSTRUCTIVE OLD FOLKS ENTERTAINING
SIMPLE SURE READY RELIABLE
PROJECTS ON THE SCREEN A PICTURE 8 FEET
PRODUCES PRETTY PRISMATIC PICTURES PLEASING TO ALL

The body of the **Electro Radiant** is a cone-sh which gathers each divergent ray of light and concent on the main reflector whence the whole mass of br

10

SPOTLIGHT ON
The father of modern advertising

Thomas Barratt was just 24 years old when he became a partner in the Pears soap company in 1865. The company's annual advertising budget was £80. Barratt created a series of catchy advertisements which helped the company grow enormously through the rest of the century. His campaigns included using the painting *Bubbles* by Sir John Everett Millais, which became the most famous poster in the country. He also persuaded famous people to recommend his soap as good for the skin. In 1897 he began publishing *Pears Shilling Cyclopaedia* every year. Many millions of copies have been sold and it is still in print today. Barratt eventually gained full control of the company, and increased spending on advertising to about £130,000. He believed that every penny was well spent because, as he stated more than once in public: 'any fool can make soap; it takes a clever man to sell it.'

Thomas Barratt used a popular painting by one of Britain's most famous painters as the heart of the Pears advertising strategy.

twentieth century. People soon became used to hearing advertisements on the radio and seeing them in cinemas, on television and on the Internet. Today, manufacturers no longer dominate the world of advertising. Modern agencies are experienced in getting the message across from what might have once been unlikely clients: government departments, charity organizations, political candidates and even religious denominations.

A campaign begins

Companies advertise themselves or their products for many reasons. A new company might be introducing itself to the public, and showing how it is different from competitors. A well established company might want to reach a new group, such as women or young people. Or it might be encouraging people to continue to buy its products or use its services. Advertising – getting a message across – is useful in all these situations.

Executives at Tokyo's Dentsu Advertising Agency check on the progress of advertisements for one of their clients – Salomon ski racing equipment.

Agencies and markets

Companies and organizations rarely take on the job of advertising themselves. Instead they turn to specialist advertising companies, called agencies, to take on the job. Some advertising agencies are locally based, catering to large and small companies in a particular city or region. Others are huge companies which employ hundreds of people in offices around the world.

SPOTLIGHT ON
Inside an agency

Major ad campaigns cost enormous amounts of money and involve hundreds of people. This is how most big advertising agencies are structured.

ACCOUNT MANAGERS
These people have the most responsibility and act as links between the client and the agency. They need to understand a client's needs and convey that information to the others in the agency. They also report back to the client on progress and present the finished product.

CREATIVES
This group of people does the thinking behind an advertisement campaign. Copywriters must fit their words to the visual ideas developed by art directors. Both groups need to understand both the client's wishes and the taste and opinion of the target audience.

STRATEGIC PLANNERS
These members of the team study different audiences and markets, and then tell the creatives how to focus their message accurately and clearly.

MEDIA BUYERS
This important group deals with newspapers, magazines, television networks and other media running advertisements. A successful media buyer can use influence to make a good deal for the agency (and therefore the client).

The link between the agency and its client (the company) is important, creating ties that can last for decades. For example, many observers believe that the contribution of the Saatchi & Saatchi advertising agency helped Britain's Conservative Party win a surprise victory in the 1979 general election. The governing Labour party was expected to win, but unemployment was rising. Conservative advertisements showed long queues of sad, unemployed people over the slogan 'Labour isn't working'. Maurice Saatchi went on to become chairman of the Conservative Party from 2003 to 2005.

Staying on message

A memorable slogan gives an important advantage, but an advertising agency needs to use it as part of a wider campaign. Deciding on how a campaign should work starts with discussions with the client, with frequent contact to make sure the agency's ideas stay close to the client's wishes. A campaign can last for a long time, aiming all the time to influence how people view the company and its products, so it is important to get things right.

A number of questions become crucial. First of all, what is the target audience? In other words, who will the advertisements be aimed at? Are these people young or old, rich or poor, male or female? For example, an advertisement for an expensive car will look different from one selling trainers.

The agency and client then need to agree on what they want to say, how they want to say it – and how often. These issues relate to the language used in advertising (see pages 20-23), as well as the budget available. Huge companies spend millions of pounds over several years repeating similar slogans in newspaper and magazine ads, radio and television commercials, on the Internet and on their own labels.

Some advertising campaigns aim to change the way people view the company or organization behind them. For example, during the 1970s and 1980s Britain's Labour Party became linked in many voters' opinion to strikes, inefficiency and extreme political views. Tony Blair repackaged the Labour Party as New Labour just months after he became leader in 1994. The 'new' was important as it put distance between his political ideas and those which voters linked to extremism and failure. New Labour went on to win the next three general elections – in 1997, 2001 and 2005.

Opposite: Britain's former prime minister Tony Blair addresses the Labour Party conference in 2005. Blair helped the Labour Party to shed its old-fashioned image by renaming it New Labour and devising a new symbol – a red rose.

THE FUTURE UP IN SMOKE?

IMAGINE YOU ARE IN CHARGE OF A NEW ADVERTISING AGENCY WHICH NEEDS ONE BIG CLIENT TO MAKE MONEY AND ESTABLISH ITSELF. COMPANY EXPENSES ARE HUGE (RENTING OFFICES, ENTERTAINING CLIENTS, PAYING EMPLOYEES, AND SO ON) BUT INCOME IS LOW. YOU ARE CONTACTED BY A MAJOR TOBACCO COMPANY OFFERING A FIVE-YEAR CAMPAIGN ADVERTISING THEIR TOP-SELLING CIGARETTE. YOU DISAPPROVE OF CIGARETTES AND KNOW SEVERAL PEOPLE WHO DIED AS A RESULT OF SMOKING, BUT THE COMPANY'S FUTURE MIGHT DEPEND ON YOUR DECISION. WHAT WOULD YOU DO?

Over
to
YOU

Releasing the message

Many of us buy items, such as cinema tickets, drinks or magazines, without thinking much about why we chose the way we did. An advertising expert might suggest that we had been persuaded that a film was worth seeing, that one brand of soft drink tasted better than others and that one magazine was more interesting than others on the shelf. All these decisions can be traced to successful advertising.

SPOTLIGHT ON Advertising space or space advertising?

Advertisers are constantly looking for new ways to display their work. People have become familiar with football kits advertising mobile phones or computers, with hardly any mention of the team. Internet security systems promise to prevent unwanted pop-up ads from dominating computer screens. Ads are commonplace on the sides of buses or on theatre programmes. But in 1993 an American advertising company proposed launching ads where no ad had been before – in space.

Space Marketing Inc, based in the state of Georgia, planned to launch 2.4 sq km billboards in orbit around the Earth. Each one would look as large as a full moon. Mike Lawson, chief executive officer of Space Marketing Inc, said that these space advertisements would be 'a tremendous opportunity for a global-oriented company to have their logo and message seen by billions of people on a history-making, high profile advertising vehicle'.

The plan produced a storm of protest in the United States and beyond. Astronomers and environmentalists joined forces with ordinary people who wanted the skies to remain pure. These protests helped the US pass a law banning 'obtrusive space advertising' in 2000.

Opposite: an American astronaut jokes for the camera outside the Space Shuttle. The joke could become reality if the United States passes a proposed new law to allow advertising on space vehicles.

People who do not work in advertising believe that advertising success is often the result of luck or genius – saying the right thing at the right time. The agency representing the De Beers diamond company came up with the slogan 'A diamond is forever' in 1947; today it is part of the English language (and De Beers continues to profit from it).

The truth is that successful advertising is like inventor Thomas Edison's definition of genius: one per cent inspiration and ninety-nine per cent perspiration. Agencies work long and hard to find the right images, words, audience and outlets for their ad campaigns.

It might seem obvious to us now that diamonds do seem to last forever: they are one of the hardest natural objects and they appear indestructible. But in 1947, when many countries were finding times hard after the Second World War, luxury goods such as diamonds seemed to be extravagances for many people – unless they felt that they were somehow buying a gift for future generations as well.

People need to be aware that advertisers try to create markets (groups of people who will buy the advertised products). Britain in 1947 probably had very few millionaires thinking of buying diamonds. But it did have millions of hard-working people who were prepared to save or budget to afford some luxury in their lives. Advertising persuaded them to make that choice. Advertisers continue to persuade us hundreds of times a day.

TALKING HEADS

THE PREGNANT MAN

One of the most famous images of the twentieth century was an advertisement that showed a man in a jumper, looking unhappily at the camera while he rubbed his swollen belly. Below the photograph was the headline: 'Would you be more careful if it was you that got pregnant?' The UK Health Education Council sponsored the advertisement as part of its drive to make men take more responsibility for contraception. Jeremy Sinclair of the Saatchi & Saatchi agency came up with the idea.

John Hegarty, who was the agency's deputy creative director at the time, had also been trying to come up with a startling image. When he saw an early version of Sinclair's idea, he was astounded: 'I almost died. It was the best thing that I had ever seen... The pregnant man was more than just a piece of advertising; it was the first time that I had seen a piece of work that moved beyond the accepted boundaries our business operated in, commanding attention from a far wider group of people.'

The message of the 'pregnant man' advertisement gained enormous publicity for its client, the UK Health Education Council. The cleverness of the ad helped to turn Saatchi & Saatchi into one of the world's most successful advertising agencies.

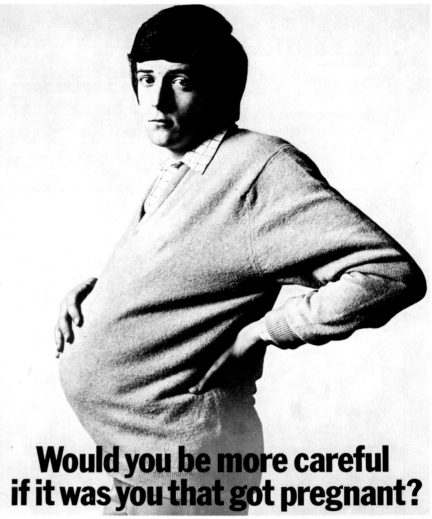

Would you be more careful if it was you that got pregnant?

It's a lot easier for a man to have a baby than for a woman.
She's the one who has to hump it around for nine months.
She's the one who has to grin and bear it. Backache, morning sickness and all.
It's not a lot of fun being pregnant, if you don't want the baby. It's not a lot of fun being an unwanted baby, either.

The Health Education Council

Anyone married or single, can get advice on contraception, from their local family planning clinic.

Over to YOU

SETTING LIMITS

THE UNITED STATES BANNED OBTRUSIVE SPACE ADVERTISING AFTER THE EPISODE OF THE ORBITING BILLBOARDS. CAN YOU THINK OF SOMEWHERE ELSE THAT SHOULD BE KEPT FREE OF ADVERTISING? WHO SHOULD DECIDE ON SUCH A BAN? WHO SHOULD ENFORCE SUCH LAWS?

New and improved

The world of advertising has its own way of expressing things, almost as though advertisers use a different language. Fiction and poetry also use language in special ways; readers take pleasure in the way the writing style of a novel or poem reveals itself. But people approach literature in a very different way from the way they view advertising.

Readers choose what they want to read, and if they find the language difficult they can read more slowly or even reread passages until they understand what they are reading. Advertisers know that they are up against a major disadvantage, which is that most people do not choose to read advertisements. Whether they flick past the ads in a colour

supplement or change channels when a television programme has an ad break, most people try to ignore advertising. The advertiser's job is to make people stop, look and listen – and that takes special skills.

Understanding the market

Advertisers constantly try to understand and influence the large number of people who might possibly buy a product – in other words, the market. They also know that people usually choose a product for one of two reasons:

- it is cheaper than others like it; or
- it is better than those of competitors.

Advertisements usually focus on just one of these benefits, and advertisers need to know which benefit is more important to their market. Not many people, for example, choose a champagne because it is the cheapest. Similarly, most buyers do not look for the best-quality paper clip – they are more likely to look for the cheapest.

Occasionally, companies can create a market and then sell these people the company's product. Think of all the different types of shampoo for sale. Some people might never have realized that they had split ends, dry hair and dandruff all at once – until a shampoo commercial told them about this condition and what to buy to make it better. Changing an existing product so that it is 'new and improved' can draw back customers who may have begun to wonder why they keep buying the product.

Opposite: pennants, flags and offers of enormous savings in this American used-car sales lot are typical of the hard sell approach to advertising.

Hard sell or soft sell?

Having studied the market, the advertising agency and client need to decide the approach to adopt in a campaign. Should they bombard people with information, constantly repeating the product name and one or two of its advantages? Or should they create a pleasant atmosphere, luring the public into the ad in a way that links the product with that good feeling? These two approaches are known as the hard sell and the soft sell. A typical hard-sell advertisement in a newspaper might be one for a three-day sale at a local supermarket. The name of the supermarket is large and unmissable in the ad. The rest of the ad has eye-catching phrases such as 'low, low prices', 'while stocks last' and 'unbeatable value'.

Television and radio commercials sometimes use the hard-sell strategy. Think of commercials for leather sofas or computer equipment that seem to shout from the television. The hard sell is not subtle. And even if most people groan when they see or hear such advertising, the message sinks in often enough to encourage advertisers to use the approach again and again.

TALKING HEADS

DIFFERENT CULTURES

Experts and the general public alike agree that British advertising is often funnier and less concerned with the hard sell than the American version. Trying to work out why this is so, some people conclude that the reason lies in the media industries on either side of the Atlantic. Because the film-making and television industries in America are so much larger, it is easier for creative film-makers to find work in those fields. In Britain, according to this argument, clever, witty film-makers need to make commercials as a way of breaking into cinema or television.

Andrew ASC Ehrenberg, the former director of the Centre for Marketing and Communications at the London Business School, takes a different view. He believes the difference lies in the way people in these countries view advertising: 'There is a public view in the US that advertising is a very powerful force, so the hard sell is more common there. Here, it is widely accepted that advertising is a very weak force and exists to reinforce existing attitudes rather than to persuade people of things they didn't believe before. That's why it tries to be so entertaining.'

The soft sell approach, on the other hand, seems deliberately to ignore some of the unspoken rules of advertising. A printed ad of this type might show a happy couple or a group of friends enjoying each other's company. Visible in the ad, but not dominating it, will be the company logo. Soft-sell commercials also draw in people by linking a product with a sense of warmth or comfort. Puppies, for example, have very little to do with toilet tissue, but many people associate toilet tissue with a particular breed of cuddly dog (and buy that brand because of it).

What could be a softer sell ad campaign for toilet paper than one showing the cuddliest puppy viewers could imagine?

IMPROVED?

TRY TO THINK OF FIVE PRODUCTS THAT YOU HAVE SEEN ADVERTISED AS 'NEW' OR 'IMPROVED' – OR MAYBE BOTH. HAVE YOU OR YOUR FAMILY BOUGHT MORE OF THEM, OR BOUGHT THEM MORE OFTEN, THAN BEFORE THOSE WORDS APPEARED ON THE LABELS OR IN ADVERTISEMENTS? DO YOU THINK THERE ARE ANY REAL DIFFERENCES IN THESE PRODUCTS?

Over to YOU

Blurred boundaries

Most people believe they can easily tell the difference between what is and what is not advertising. It is usually obvious which newspaper pages, or parts of a page, are advertising and which are not. In the same way, the commercial breaks during television programmes are obviously advertisements.

But can we trust our judgement? Is it possible to be confused, and read or view an advertisement that we thought was a news story? The answer to the first question seems to be 'not always' and to the second a worrying 'yes'.

THE FIRST AUSTRALIAN PERFUME.

Sheila

EAU DE PARFUM

(ALSO KILLS FLIES.)

The 1989 Sheila spoof advertising posters were so successful that many people tried to find stockists of the perfume – or insect-killer (see panel, right).

Grabbing people's attention

In 1989, the London-based advertising company More O'Ferrall developed a new type of lightweight bus shelter panel, which could display advertising posters. These panels aimed to attract the attention of people outside the shelter – mainly motorists driving past – rather than the people waiting inside.

Some experts felt that drivers would pay no attention to these panels. So the people at More O'Ferrall came up with an unusual plan to win over the doubters: they advertised a fake product and promised that people would be talking about it within days. The product would not be advertised anywhere else, to test the effectiveness of the panels.

More O'Ferrall used 4500 of their 30,000 panels around Britain to advertise Sheila. The ad showed a normal-looking perfume bottle, but with an outback-style hat instead of the usual lid. Next to it was the headline: 'The First Australian Perfume'. And in case anyone thought that this was a real product, a second line of text at the bottom read 'Also kills flies'.

By early April, people all over the country had begun to phone radio stations, write letters to newspapers and discuss this interesting new product. Ian Orsman, who was head of the cosmetics department at Harrods Department Store in London, said, 'We've had requests coming in for it for the last week and a half. We found out that it was just an advertising stunt.' The campaign might have been just a stunt, but it proved how effectively advertisers could catch the public's imagination.

Companies constantly try to disguise advertising so that people will believe that their claims (that a product is better, cleaner, faster or cheaper) appear as fact. Some of these efforts are easy to spot. A late-night television programme about the making of an album may be a promotional film which aims to boost sales of a pop star's new release. These programmes are cheap to broadcast (as the record company has done all the filming) and gives a television station the chance to be linked to the pop star.

SPOTLIGHT ON
Product placement

When we go to the cinema, we expect to sit through a number of advertisements before the film begins. But sometimes the advertising continues right through the film itself. Films cost many millions of pounds to make, so film producers are always trying to find ways to raise money.

One method is called product placement. A film producer approaches a company and says that a new film could use that company's product (for example, a type of car, beer or pet food) in some scenes. Film-goers would see characters using these products, and the labels would be visible some of the time. In exchange, the company would pay the film producers an agreed fee.

One of the most famous examples of product placement was in the film *ET*, made in 1982. The director Steven Spielberg's film company, Amblin Productions, approached Mars Inc, the makers of M&M sweets. They offered to show the film's young characters luring ET from his spaceship with M&Ms. In exchange, Mars would advertise the film on its sweet packets. The company refused, deciding that it did not want

M&Ms associated with aliens from outer space. Spielberg's company then turned to the Hershey Company, which agreed that ET should nibble a Hershey sweet called Reese's Pieces in a similar deal. The film went on to break box-office records and sales of Reese's Pieces rose by 85 per cent.

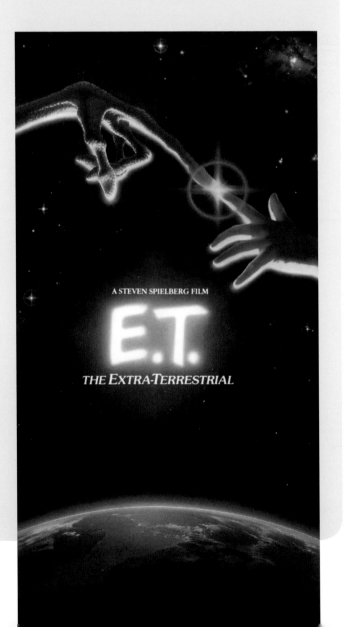

Other mixtures of fact and advertising are harder to distinguish. Newspapers and magazines often feature stories that seem – at first glance, and sometimes longer – to be news stories about the finest hotels or best cars. The typeface and headlines seem to be those used elsewhere in the publication Only the words 'advertising promotion' or 'special report' offer a clue as to who has produced the article. Journalists describe these stories or reports as advertorials. The broadcasting equivalent is called an infomercial. It is easy to see how these terms arose.

Boundaries between advertisements and the real world can become blurred in unexpected ways. Many advertising campaigns rely on slogans or catchphrases that become popular with the public. Over the years, people have taken some of these to heart, giving a boost to the advertisers and their clients. Below are some of the most popular, some of which are still used, even if the company has dropped the slogan:
'Finger-lickin' good' (KFC restaurants);
'Refreshes the parts that other beers fail to reach' (Heineken lager);
'Melts in your mouth – not in your hands' (M&M sweets);
'Just do it' (Nike sportswear);
'We try harder' (Avis car hire company).

Over to YOU

LOCAL TEST

FREE NEWSPAPERS AND MAGAZINES ARE DELIVERED REGULARLY TO HOMES IN MOST PARTS OF BRITAIN. THESE PUBLICATIONS RELY ON ADVERTISING MONEY, RATHER THAN SALES OF COPIES, TO STAY IN BUSINESS. DO YOU THINK THESE PUBLICATIONS CAN BE TRUSTED TO PROVIDE ACCURATE INFORMATION ABOUT SOME OF THE COMPANIES THEY REVIEW (SUCH AS HOTELS AND RESTAURANTS), OR DO YOU THINK THAT THE REVIEWS ARE SIMPLY A FRONT FOR PAID ADVERTISING?

Targeting youth

Young people are often described as tomorrow's leaders. Advertisers also realize that the young are tomorrow's buyers, so they devote a great deal of time and money to attracting their attention. At first glance, this strategy might seem hard to explain. Most young people have relatively little money to spend, so is youth-directed advertising something of a waste?

In fact children are highly influenced by advertising and do their best to persuade their parents to buy their favourite products, as anyone who has been to a supermarket or toy shop can confirm. Looked at in this light, children's advertising is really aimed at the adults who eventually pay for the products, with the children adding their voices to that of the advertisements.

But there is more to youth advertising than simply using children to influence their parents. Young people, like any customers, often build brand loyalty. If they start to wear a particular type of trainer when they are young, they are likely to continue buying that brand in later life. Also, when they have more spending power, they might also buy other sportswear produced by the same company.

Governments, the general public, companies and advertising agencies need to find a balance between business freedom and responsibility towards children. Ads featuring or aimed at children generate sales and provide competition (both of which are vital to national economies), but they can easily take advantage of young people.

Opposite: the McDonald's fast-food company has used the clown figure of Ronald McDonald to appeal to children since 1963. Some studies claim that he is the most recognized figure in the world after Santa Claus.

Becoming consumers

Ofcom, the UK communications watchdog (see page 37), studies commercial TV closely, especially the way in which children are exposed to – and come to understand – television advertising. Their research points to the following pattern of development.

• Most children younger than four or five view advertising simply as entertainment and make little or no connection with the product.

• Between the ages of four and seven, children begin to distinguish between ordinary programmes and advertising.

• By the age of eight, most children realize that commercials are trying to persuade them to do or buy something.

• When children enter their teens they begin to engage with the content of commercials. They listen to the message and decide whether or not they are persuaded.

Because younger children are less concerned with the details of a commercial message, advertisers make ads at a level at which children can become involved. That means using bright colours, lively music, animation and cartoon characters. This type of advertising is hardly the best preparation for developing a critical sense, as it aims to hide any message beneath the entertainment.

TALKING HEADS

NETTING PROFITS

As broadcasting regulations on children's television advertising become stronger, some companies are targeting popular children's websites with their ads. Michael Smith, of the British Internet company MindCandy, understands the temptation that these companies face: 'There are a lot of concerns about advertising to children in these places. The way you can connect with kids is so much more powerful online. It's going to be tough for people to resist the lure of advertising money.'

Over to YOU

STERNER LIMITS?

CHILDREN'S ADVERTISING COMES UNDER STRICTER CONTROLS EVERY YEAR IN BRITAIN AND OTHER DEVELOPED COUNTRIES. TELEVISION ADVERTISERS ARE TOLD WHAT AND HOW THEY CAN ADVERTISE AT TIMES WHEN CHILDREN ARE WATCHING. YET MANY OF THE PROBLEMS THAT ADVERTISING CONTROLS TRY TO GUARD AGAINST – SUCH AS CHILDHOOD OBESITY RESULTING FROM EATING TOO MUCH JUNK FOOD – CONTINUE TO INCREASE. DO YOU THINK THE ANSWER IS TO BAN ALL ADVERTISING FROM CHILDREN'S TELEVISION?

SPOTLIGHT ON
The power of the Internet

Young people are not simply targets for skilled advertisers out for a profit. With their technology skills, they are often the first to use new forms of communication to their advantage. An excellent case in point is the 'Yes We Can' video that swept the Internet in early 2008.

'Yes We Can' is a highly successful example of viral advertising (see page 40), supporting the American presidential candidate Barack Obama. Much of Obama's support comes from young people, who echo his calls for sweeping change in the way politics operates. Obama supporters display posters with the slogan 'Yes We Can', referring to the chanting that often accompanies his speeches.

Hip hop artist Will.i.am (right) took four and a half minutes of an Obama speech and composed a song to accompany the candidate's words. He and other Obama supporters – including Scarlett Johansson, John Legend, Aisha Tyler, Nick Cannon and Amber Valletta – sang or recited parts of the speech, returning again and again to the repeated phrase 'yes we can'.

The 'Yes We Can' video shows how the Internet can be an immediate – and cheap – way to advertise. Will.i.am thought of it on 29 January and had it finished and uploaded to the YouTube video site by 2 February. It has been viewed millions of times on the site, and at one point was getting a million hits a day.

Going too far?

The advertising industry constantly finds itself in the midst of controversy. Sometimes being controversial can be helpful: some advertisers might cite the old saying that there is no such thing as bad publicity. An extreme example of someone who held this view is P T Barnum, the nineteeth century American showman. He once said of his critics: 'I don't care what they say about me as long as they spell my name right.'

P.T. BARNUM & CO'S GREATEST SHOW ON EARTH & THE GREAT LONDON CIRCUS COMBINED WITH

GREAT JUMBO'S SKELETON

P.T.BARNUM.

JUMBO.

THE COLOSSAL PRODIGIOUS FRAME of the LARGEST and NOBLEST Animal that ever lived. The ONLY ELEPHANT SKELETON ever publicly exhibited. A STRANGE & AMAZING SHOW WITHOUT A PARELLEL. MOUNTED BY PROF. HENRY A. WARD, THE DISTINGUISHED NATURALIST & SCIENTIST of ROCHESTER, N.Y.

SANGERS ROYAL BRITISH MENAGERIE & GRAND INTERNATIONAL SHOWS

As a rule, advertisers know they must take care not to turn public opinion against them or the products they advertise. In the age of instant communication a consumer backlash can spread quickly – through e-mail, text messaging and community websites. If a company or advertiser is caught behaving in an unethical way, the bad publicity may last years.

How far is too far?

If P T Barnum's view of publicity is true, then why should advertisers and their clients care about what people think? After all, advertisers are paid to get people's attention and – if all goes well – to keep it. If there is something a little naughty or edgy in doing just that, then who can really complain?

Opposite: American showman P T Barnum was proud of the weird and exotic exhibits he displayed. For years, the main circus attraction was Jumbo, the largest elephant on Earth. Even after Jumbo's death in 1885, Barnum used the elephant's skeleton to attract customers.

The answer is that companies keep a close eye on the people who make up their market. If even a part of that group – people wearing glasses, curly-haired children, dog lovers – feel offended by an advertisement, then those people might choose to buy a rival product. And if they feel strongly enough, they might mount effective public campaigns against the company or its product.

Advertising thrives in countries that have a strong tradition of free speech, so it can be difficult to impose legal restrictions on what can or cannot be said in an advertisement. People with complaints can use some of the same legal actions that apply to any print or broadcasting. For example, a company can be taken to court if an advertisement contains a libel or if it encourages illegal behaviour. If an advertisement makes a dishonest claim about a product – for example, how effective a diet pill might be – the agency or parent company could also face legal action.

SPOTLIGHT ON
The Marlboro Man

Fifty-one-year-old Wayne McLaren died of lung cancer in Newport Beach, California in 1992. During his last years, McLaren had been an anti-smoking campaigner. His cancer almost certainly developed because of the 25 years he was a regular smoker. McLaren's death was not so unusual – about four million people die every year as a result of smoking-related illness.

What made McLaren's death noteworthy was his past. Many people remember him as the Marlboro Man, who featured in advertisements for Marlboro cigarettes. At first, the cigarettes were marketed for women. But, from the early 1950s, advertisements showed the Marlboro Man – usually a cowboy, hunter or other masculine role model – smoking a Marlboro cigarette.

Wayne McLaren was one of many different men who were used as models for the Marlboro Man. The advertising campaign was familiar around the world, which is why McLaren's illness and death received so much publicity. McLaren spent much of his last year campaigning against cigarettes – and especially against tobacco advertising. One of the last things he said was: 'Take care of the children. Tobacco will kill you, and I am living proof of it.'

The social cost

Most advertising steers away from being illegal. But that might not be enough to keep advertisers in the clear. The reputation of a company can be damaged if some of its advertising claims are proved legally to be false. But a company could find itself with a steeper uphill battle if its advertising is linked to attitudes that society frowns on.

Today, few agencies would produce advertisements of the sort that were common in the 1980s. Many ads at that time appeared to promote an aggressive, win-at-all-costs attitude to life. Likewise, modern consumers are offended by ads that seem to reinforce racial or gender stereotypes. Concerns about social justice, religious freedom

and the environment lie behind many people's reaction to advertising nowadays. There is little chance of an advertiser being charged with supporting environmentally wasteful behaviour. But people will make up their own minds about supporting such a company.

The Marlboro Man advertisements aimed to generate new sales by linking the cigarette with the rugged men of America's West.

Over to YOU

PROTEST LIST
SEE IF YOU CAN LIST FIVE ADVERTISEMENTS (FROM TELEVISION, MAGAZINES OR THE INTERNET) THAT YOU CONSIDER MISLEADING OR OFFENSIVE. ASK A FRIEND TO DO THE SAME AND THEN EXCHANGE LISTS. WAS ANY AD ON BOTH LISTS? DID YOU FIND THAT YOU AND YOUR FRIEND AGREED ON WHAT COUNTED AS 'GOING TOO FAR'?

Advertising watchdogs

If a family paid an electrician to rewire their house and the wiring led to a damaging house fire, they would probably take the electrician to court. They had a legal agreement with the electrician to pay for a job done well and to recognized safety standards. Similarly, a driver would expect some sort of compensation from a garage if a wheel they had replaced fell off at high speed.

The consumers in the cases above would have known that professional organizations set standards for electricians, car mechanics and many other trades. Members of these organizations must meet these standards in all their work: otherwise they might be taken to court or punished in some other way.

Who is to blame?

The advertising industry must also be prepared to face criticism and complaints from the public. Misleading, demeaning and false advertising can stir up trouble from the very groups the advertising is targeting (see pages 32-35).

Advertising restrictions aim to keep alcohol, tobacco and other dangerous substances away from young people.

The question is, who is responsible for advertisements: the companies advertising the products or the agencies they employ? The advertising industry, in Britain and in many other countries, recognizes that the government could draft and enforce strict regulations if it does not take responsibility for its work. This recognition led to the creation of the Advertising Standards Authority (ASA) in the UK and to similar bodies in other countries.

Consumers can complain directly to the ASA, which examines the complaint and reaches a decision on whether an offending ad should be banned. The argument against this system of self-regulation is that complaints can only be made, and offensive advertising stopped, after an offence has been caused. However, the ASA does work with other organizations which check print, radio and television advertisements before they are released.

The broadest coverage

The ASA and groups like it also act as watchdogs in monitoring companies which produce advertising that comes under government control. For example, tobacco advertising is banned in many areas, alcohol advertising is strictly controlled and children's advertising constantly faces new regulations.

Organizations that act as advertising watchdogs often work in partnership with other groups dealing with wider broadcasting issues. In the UK, for example, the Ofcom watchdog oversees broadcasting on radio and television. Some of that broadcasting is advertising, so Ofcom acts alongside the ASA in keeping the industry fair and respectable.

Over to YOU

DOES THE SYSTEM WORK?

DO YOU THINK THAT A SYSTEM OF ADVERTISING SELF-REGULATION, SUCH AS THE ONE IN THE UK, WORKS OR SHOULD THE GOVERNMENT DO MORE TO CONTROL ADVERTISING? WHAT ARE THE ARGUMENTS FOR AND AGAINST ANY CHANGE TO THE SYSTEM?

The final analysis

In 1957, the American journalist and social critic Vance Packard published *The Hidden Persuaders*, a book which examined the advertising industry. Until then, Americans had accepted advertising as a fact of life, something that – like the weather – was always around but that they could not do anything about.

Packard turned his attention to many things we now accept, but which seemed revolutionary at the time. Without overloading his book with statistics and footnotes, he gave people an insight into how the advertising industry works. Some of what Packard wrote

has dated over the past 50 or so years. For example, he appeared to think that housewives could be almost hypnotized by some sorts of advertising. He did, however, open people's eyes to how the industry worked and how advertising affects people generally. In that respect, Packard's contribution has been enormous. Nowadays people spend their entire careers analysing advertising. Even more importantly, consumers have become far more aware of how advertising works – and many have used this knowledge to their own advantage.

Clued up

Twenty-first century consumers are far more aware of the media than their counterparts in the 1950s. Advertising finds its way into nearly every area of the media – from traditional newspaper classifieds to cold-calling telephone advertising to web pop-ups and banners and viral marketing (see page 40).

Opposite: huge call centres in India provide countries in the English-speaking world with a pool of capable workers who can deal with telephone business. They are linked to those countries via modern communications systems. Call centres also enable advertisers to use cold-calling techniques, phoning people at home to sell them products or services.

Today people – and especially young people – are bombarded by advertisements throughout their lives. These can be heeded or ignored if people have the skills to identify the advertising for what it is. Some people may be especially vulnerable to these increasingly sophisticated attempts to influence their behaviour, especially young and very old people. Governments often try to build safeguards into commercial deals, so that fewer people suffer as a result of being misled. For example, many financial contracts (for purchases, insurance or investments) have 'cooling off' periods during which buyers have a chance to seek advice if they feel they were rushed into a deal, or if they were misled.

Other young people, on the other hand, have shown that they can turn the system on its head. By using the same technology and communications developments that helped advertising evolve (especially mobile phones and the Internet) they can send out alternative messages – for social change, against the power of big companies or simply to publicize themselves and their projects.

SPOTLIGHT ON
Viral advertising

Experts on advertising and marketing are always on the lookout for new trends. One of the most successful recent forms of promoting ideas – known as viral marketing or viral advertising – combines new technology and old-fashioned word of mouth. People spread the word about a film, book, band or album by text message, e-mail or on social websites. Viral advertising has two main advantages. It taps into modern communication technology, so it can target thousands of people instantly and at low cost. Links to the web and mobile phone networks help to give viral advertising its edgy, up-to-the-minute feel. This is what prompts people to forward viral ads on to their friends.

Some of the most successful examples ignored traditional advertising strategies altogether. *The Blair Witch Project*, a low-budget horror film, became incredibly popular after its release in 1999 because news and clips from it were released on the web. Made for £18,000, the film has gone on to earn nearly £127 million.

The Arctic Monkeys, the band from Sheffield, also used viral marketing to become popular. The band approved of fans who uploaded versions of their songs on to community websites. More than 140 versions of some Arctic Monkeys songs were on the net – and the band was selling out concert venues – before the first official single was released in 2005. The Arctic Monkeys have gone on to become one of Britain's most popular bands, headlining at the Glastonbury Festival and winning several BRIT awards.

Traditional companies and agencies also use viral techniques. The chocolates made by Cadbury had become less popular from 2006-7, and the company decided it needed to rebuild its image. In November 2006, it stopped sponsoring the TV soap *Coronation Street*, which it felt was old-fashioned. Instead, Cadbury concentrated on a gorilla campaign aimed at young people. The main ad in this campaign showed a gorilla listening to music and then joining in on a crazy drum solo. Only at this point did the Cadbury logo appear on screen. The ad has run on television and in cinemas; Cadbury has also uploaded it – in true viral style – to MySpace and other community websites.

The Arctic Monkeys were a top band on the Glastonbury Pyramid Stage in 2007, only two years after they released their first single.

Over to YOU

DIY CAMPAIGNS

TRY TO THINK OF HOW YOU MIGHT ADVERTISE A NEW TYPE OF RUNNING SHOE, A CHARITY HELPING BLIND PEOPLE, A POP FESTIVAL, A NEW FLAVOUR OF ICE-CREAM AND AN ENVIRONMENTALLY FRIENDLY CAR. WHICH TYPE OF ADVERTISING WOULD YOU USE FOR EACH CAMPAIGN? COULD YOU USE A SIMILAR TECHNIQUE FOR ALL OF THEM? WHAT FACTORS WOULD INFLUENCE THE TYPE OF ADVERTISING YOU WOULD CHOOSE?

The shape of the future

What is the future of advertising in this Internet age? The 1982 sci-fi film *Blade Runner* was set in 2019 and offered a bleak view of an overcrowded Earth, with menacing lifelike robots, skies darkened by pollution and advertising everywhere – including on airships floating above the city.

This is a disturbing extension of the idea of advertising in space (see page 16). The film-makers intended audiences to feel uncomfortable about a world dominated by advertising. Some of the developments the film portrayed are already happening: do they offer consumers more freedom or less privacy?

Advertisers are always trying to reach their target audience at the least cost. Thousands of people every day see the giant billboards in London's Piccadilly Circus or New York's Times Square. Even the sci-fi airship advertising of

Advertisers might try to reach the youth market by sending advertisements to mobile phones. Phone users receiving the ads would be charged less for calls and texts.

Blade Runner might soon be a reality. The problem with this type of advertising is that it is expensive and that its content is not automatically noticed by people walking by every day.

This is why many advertisers are looking to a future where 'less is more'. By focusing on a smaller group – but knowing that these people will actually see the ads – advertising companies can cut costs and achieve a higher success rate. Techniques being developed today signal how the advertising industry could look in 10 or 20 years.

Organizations already track the ways in which people use the Internet, passing on information to companies that fit the same profile. If someone, for example, spends a lot of time looking at sport websites, he or she might begin receiving e-mails or seeing pop-up ads from companies which make trainers, sports equipment or which sell tickets to popular sporting events.

A fair deal?

Other companies are beginning to offer advertising as a way of helping consumers to cut costs or to afford new technology. Mobile phone companies already offer deals which slash phone charges – as long as the customer is willing to receive ads broadcast over the phone. These deals are targeted mainly at young phone users, who have less money to spend.

The American company Accenture has found another way to weave advertising into the fabric of people's lives. It is developing technology to help people turn their digital photos into slide shows that can appear on screens anywhere in the house. The catch? The same software enables Accenture to slip advertising into some of the family photos.

As always, advertising continues to bewitch and offer glimpses of worlds that people want to visit. In the past, people have been able to control what they were presented with – by flipping a page or by changing the channel on the television. Will people still have that freedom in the future?

Glossary

advertorial   A newspaper advertisement that looks like a normal news story.

agency   A company that produces advertising.

brand loyalty   Buying a particular make of product again and again.

BRIT   The British Recording Industry Trust, which sponsors annual pop-music awards in the UK.

classified advertising   Small newspaper or magazine advertisements, usually just a few lines of text.

cold-calling   Phoning strangers to advertise something.

consumer   Someone who buys things.

critical   Relating to the skill of judging the real meaning (of, for example, advertisements).

demeaning   Portraying individuals or a group of people in a negative way.

developed countries   Richer countries whose people have more money to spend.

engage   To respond to something with full understanding.

environmentalist   Someone who supports efforts to protect the Earth.

extravagance   An unnecessary luxury item.

free speech   The basic right to say what you want without being arrested.

glossy   Expensively produced.

Industrial Revolution   A period which began in Britain in the 1700s, when goods began to be manufactured in factories rather than by hand.

infomercial   A radio or television advertisement that resembles a normal programme.

investment   A way of using money in the hope of making more money.

libel   An untruth about a person that is printed in a publication.

logo   The visual symbol of a company.

mass-produced   Manufactured in large numbers by machine, rather than by hand.

media   The different forms of mass communication, including print, radio and television.

obtrusive   Unwanted and obvious.

orbit   A circular path around a planet.

Second World War   The war which lasted from 1939 to 1945 in which Germany, Japan, Italy and their allies fought the UK, the United States, China and their allies.

self-regulating   Not relying on the government to impose controls and restrictions.

stereotype   An oversimplified and often biased depiction of a group of people.

unemployment   Being without a job.

unethical   Deliberately wrong.

Further reading

Advertising (Behind the Media) Catherine Chambers (Heinemann, 2001)

Advertising and Marketplace (Influence and Persuasion) Clive Gifford (Heinemann, 2005)

The Hidden Persuaders Vance Packard (Ig Publishing, 2007 reissued edition)

Advertising (Mediawise) Julian Petley (Hodder Wayland, 2002)

Creative Advertising: Ideas and Techniques from the World's Best Campaigns Mario Pricken
(Thames & Hudson, 2004)

Website links

The Advertising Association

www.adassoc.org.uk

Advertising Standards Authority

www.asa.org.uk

The Incorporated Society of British Advertisers (ISBA)

www.isba.org.uk

MediaSmart

www.mediasmart.org.uk

Ofcom

www.ofcom.org.uk

http://www.buynothingday.co.uk/

http://pbskids.org/dontbuyit/

Index

QUACK!

Phyllis Root

illustrated by Holly Meade

WALKER BOOKS
AND SUBSIDIARIES

LONDON · BOSTON · SYDNEY · AUCKLAND

Mama Duck calls

quack quack quack!

Ducklings hatching

crack

Baby ducklings
in a heap
tumble out

Ducklings waddle.
Ducklings trip.

Duckling wings go

flip flap flip!

Wherever Mama goes
they go –

baby ducklings
in a row.

Baby ducklings
nip and
nibble.

Duckling
tails go
wobble,
wibble.

Baby ducklings in a dash

find a puddle ...

Contents

The First Cities

Mesopotamia is a Greek word, meaning 'the land between the rivers'. These rivers are the Tigris and the Euphrates, which wind their way south from the mountains of what is now eastern Turkey, and across the flat plains of present-day Iraq, until they pour into the Persian Gulf.

Mesopotamia is part of the 'fertile crescent', a curve of land stretching from the Persian Gulf north and west to the Mediterranean Sea. It was here, more than ten thousand years ago, that people, for the first time ever, learned to produce their food by farming. Instead of moving from place to place, hunting animals and gathering wild plant foods, they settled down, growing crops and keeping sheep and cattle. In one part of the fertile crescent, Mesopotamia, villages grew into towns and then cities, the first in the world. It was in these cities that writing, kingship, temples, irrigation, bronze-making, written laws, and many other features of later civilizations were invented.

WEBLINK
http://www.mesopotamia.co.uk

A good general site on Mesopotamian civilisation, from the British Museum.

MESOPOTAMIA
This map shows the major cities of the Mesopotamian civilization, as well as the Tigris and Euphrates rivers, which have shifted their courses many times throughout history.

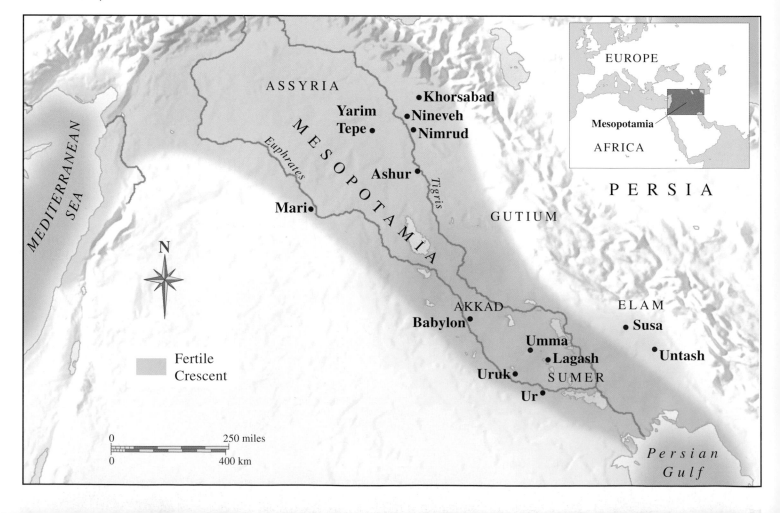

HOW DO WE KNOW?

For thousands of years, early Mesopotamian history was forgotten about. The only signs that the civilization had ever existed were large earth mounds, called tells, which stood out against the plains. Tells were formed over thousands of years, from fallen buildings made of dried mud bricks and other rubbish left behind by ancient people. From the early nineteenth century, European travellers began to dig into the tells. They found the ruins of ancient palaces and temples, together with sculpture, pottery and other treasures. They had rediscovered the world's first cities.

Over time, many different peoples speaking different languages lived in the Mesopotamian area.

The civilization was created around 4000BCE by people who lived in a region called Sumer, in southern Mesopotamia. These people were the Sumerians, who built the first cities, such as Ur and Uruk. Around 2350BCE, Sumer was conquered by Sargon, king of Akkad, the region to the north, who created the world's first empire. Akkadian, a language related to Arabic and Hebrew, replaced Sumerian as the main language. Yet despite changes of language, the arrival of new peoples, and the rise and fall of more empires, the main features of Mesopotamian civilization, such as the writing system, continued for thousands of years.

URUK

These mounds are the remains of a great brick ziggurat, or temple tower, at Uruk, the first important Mesopotamian city. You can see how the ruins stand out against the flat desert of southern Iraq.

Irrigation and Farming

Like Egypt, where another early civilization developed, Mesopotamia is a hot country with little rain. In both countries, it was only possible to grow food thanks to the annual flooding of rivers – the Nile in Egypt and the Tigris and the Euphrates in Mesopotamia. Unlike the Nile, which flooded at the right time of year to plant crops, Mesopotamia's rivers flooded when the crops were already growing in the fields. The water had to be channelled and stored, so that later it could be used to water the fields.

In early times, people lived and farmed close to the rivers. To prevent the floods washing away their villages, they built dykes, raised mounds on the river banks. They dug canals and ditches to carry the water away from the river to reservoirs. Canals also carried water to areas which had previously been desert, allowing more and more food to be produced.

The rivers also carried silt, which was left behind after the flood season ended. To prevent the canals filling up, this silt had to be dug out regularly. This was hard work, but everyone

CANAL REPAIR
These men are cleaning the silt out of an irrigation canal, using copper-bladed shovels and baskets made of reeds. They receive their orders from a local official called a *gugallum*, or canal inspector.

WEBLINK
http://www-geology.ucdavis.edu/~GEL115/115CH17oldirrigation.html

Find out about irrigation in Mesopotamia and other ancient societies.

knew that it had to be done to stop the land returning to desert.

The most important food crops were barley and dates. Date palm trees are either male or female. Male flowers produce pollen, which female flowers use to make fruit. One male tree produces enough pollen for fifty female trees. To have plenty of dates, Mesopotamian farmers grew more female trees, cutting down most male trees for wood. Usually pollen is carried from tree to tree by insects, such as bees. With so few male trees, farmers did this job themselves.

GROWING DATES
To pollinate the date trees by hand, Mesopotamian farmers climbed ladders to put pollen from the male flowers onto the female flowers.

LARGE FARMS
Mesopotamian rulers owned great farming estates, such as the one shown on this carving, dating from around 700BCE. Houses and other buildings are in the centre, with palm trees at the bottom.

HOW DO WE KNOW?

The number and size of ruined Mesopotamian cities, in areas which are now desert, show that irrigation and farming were carried out on a massive scale. How else could the people who lived in these cities be fed? We also have the evidence of thousands of ancient dried up irrigation canals, found across the deserts of southern Iraq. More evidence comes from ancient texts concerning farming, including instructions for irrigating fields and planting and harvesting crops.

Writing

The Sumerians needed to keep records of cattle, sheep and crops. Around 3300BCE, they began to do this by drawing simple pictures on clay tablets. A picture of a bull's head was used to show cattle, while an ear of barley stood for grain. Pictures could also be used to show ideas. A drawing of a foot, for example, could stand for a journey. Over time, the style of drawing changed, with curved lines becoming groups of straight wedges, the quickest marks to make with a cut reed called a stylus. From these marks, we called Mesopotamian writing 'cuneiform' (wedge-shaped).

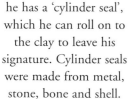

SCRIBE
A scribe writes on a soft clay tablet, using a reed stylus. Around his neck, he has a 'cylinder seal', which he can roll on to the clay to leave his signature. Cylinder seals were made from metal, stone, bone and shell.

TABLET
Many thousands of clay tablets with cuneiform writing have been found, including whole libraries, often baked hard in ancient fires. This tablet has a list of different goods. Numbers were made by pushing the blunt end of the stylus into the clay, making circles and crescents. This is an early form of cuneiform, with signs still resembling pictures.

By 3100BCE, people had realised that a sign could be used to show the sound of the word as well as the object itself. So the sign for a bull could be the sound 'gu' (bull in Sumerian), while the sign for a fish could be 'ku' (fish in Sumerian). By grouping sound signs together, people could now spell different words. In doing this, they had invented writing.

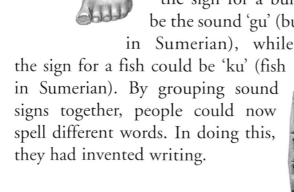

HOW DO WE KNOW?

The fact that we can read cuneiform today is largely thanks to an English scholar called Henry Rawlinson. In 1825, he found long cuneiform inscriptions carved on a high cliff face in Iran, in three ancient languages: Babylonian, Elamite and Old Persian. Rawlinson copied these, and correctly guessed that signs at the start of each text were the name of the Persian king, Darius. By trial and error, he went on to read more and more of the signs. First he deciphered the Old Persian inscription, using his knowledge of the modern form of the language. He then spent years deciphering the other two languages.

SEAL
Cylinder seals were used to sign letters and to seal jars or doors to protect valuables. This plaster impression, made by the seal on the right, shows the scribe, who is the figure on the left, being presented to a seated goddess by another goddess.

WEBLINK
http://www.
mesopotamia.co.uk/
writing/explore/exp_
main.html

Find out about the work of Mesopotamian scribes.

Cuneiform was a difficult writing system to learn. While our alphabet has just twenty-six letters, there were more than six hundred cuneiform signs. Some boys were sent to school at a young age to train to be professional writers, called scribes, but only wealthy people could afford to have their sons trained. We know about school lessons thanks to thousands of exercise tablets that have been found. These have a text written by a teacher on one side, with a pupil's copy, less skilfully done, on the other. Some of these exercises describe schoolboys' lives: 'When I rose early in the morning, I faced my mother and said to her, "Give me my lunch, I want to go to school!" My mother gave me two rolls and I set out.'

Although cuneiform was invented for record keeping, many more uses were found for it. It was used to write down laws, histories, stories, hymns, letters, scientific texts, magic spells and recipes. It continued to be used for almost 3,200 years by many different peoples across western Asia.

Craftworkers

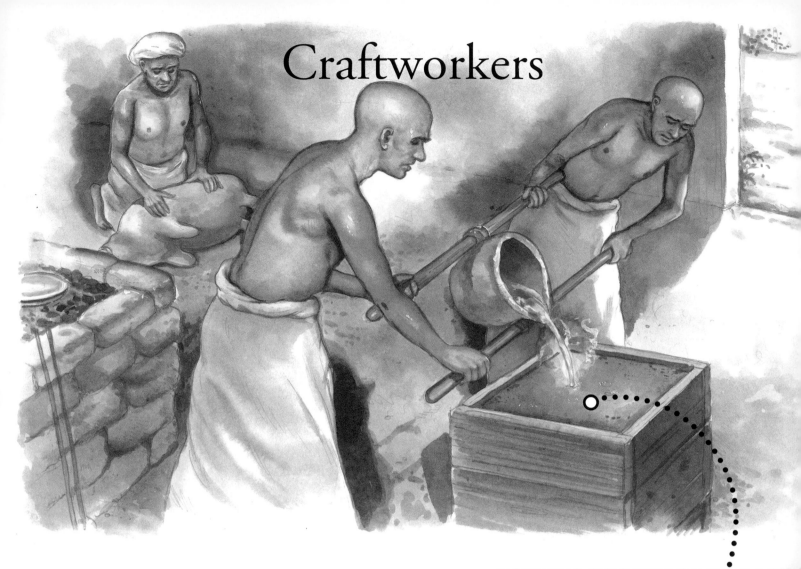

WORKSHOP
The man on the left is using skin bellows to pump air into a furnace, to make it hotter until the copper can be melted. On the right, two men pour molten copper into a mould, to make a statue.

KING'S HEAD
This head of a king, dating from 2300-2200BCE, was made from copper. It once had eyes, probably made from precious stones.

The Mesopotamians were experts at making tools, weapons and sculptures out of metal. At first, the main metal they used was copper. Then, some time before 3000BCE, they discovered that adding a small amount of tin to the copper made a new harder metal, called bronze. Bronze was much better for making tools and weapons. It also melted at a lower temperature than copper, was more fluid, and was easier to cast.

To make flat tools, such as knives, the craftworkers carved their shape on a

WEBLINK
http://www.unc.edu/
courses/rometech/
public/content/arts_and
_crafts/Sara_Malone/
BRONZE_3.html

Find out about ancient
bronze casting.

flat stone. Then they heated lumps of copper and tin together in a stone or pottery vessel, called a crucible, until they melted. The liquid bronze was then poured into the stone mould.

To make statues and bowls, the Mesopotamians invented a method called the 'lost wax' process. First they made a model out of wax, or of clay covered with wax. Clay was packed around the model to make a mould. This was heated, so that the wax melted and drained out through holes. Liquid metal was poured into the mould, filling the space left by the 'lost wax'. Once the metal had cooled and hardened, the clay mould was broken open to reveal the sculpture.

Mesopotamians were also fine potters. Some time before 4500BCE, they invented the potter's wheel, which allowed them to shape a bowl while turning it. The earliest pots were made on a slow wheel. Around 2000BCE, they invented a fast-turning wheel, which allowed them to make vessels with thinner walls in a quicker time.

POT OF TOOLS

In about 2500BCE, someone in the city of Susa, capital of Elam, buried this collection of bronze tools and other items in a pottery jar, probably for safe keeping. From the jar's shape, we can tell that it was made on a slow-turning wheel. A fast wheel would make a more regular shape.

HOW DO WE KNOW?

In any ancient site, the commonest craft item found is pottery. Unlike metal objects, which can be melted and recycled, a broken pot can only be thrown away. While wood or textiles decay, pottery will last for ever in the earth. Metal objects, such as the copper head of the king, survive more rarely. Evidence for how they were made comes from examining the objects themselves. Archaeologists have found stone moulds used to make knives, still scorched black by hot metal. The 'lost wax' method was also invented in other countries, such as China and East Africa, and is still used today.

Trade

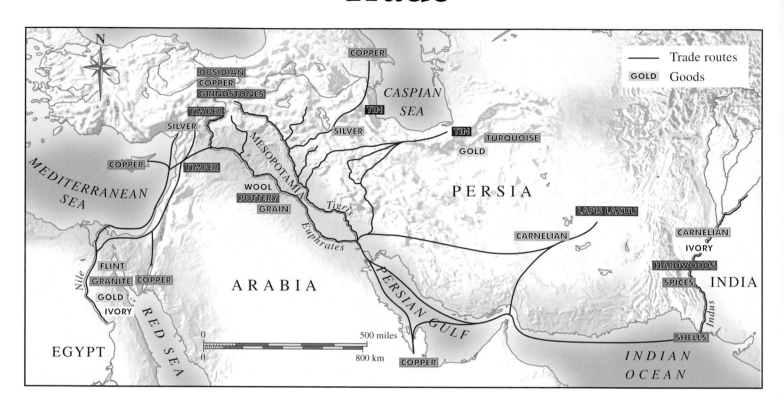

WEBLINK
http://www.
mesopotamia.co.uk/
trade/home_set.html

The British Museum's
site on trade and
transport.

Mesopotamia had plenty of clay, bitumen (natural tar), reeds and palm trees, whose wood is only good for making rough beams. The country lacked all other raw materials, such as stone, metal, and good timber for building or making furniture. So from the beginnings of Mesopotamian civilization, people had to trade with other lands to get the materials they needed.

The easiest way to transport heavy goods, such as stones, was by water, along rivers and canals and across the sea. Boats were made of bundles of reeds, waterproofed by coating them with bitumen. Reed boats are still used in Iraq today, and remains of ancient boats show that they have been built in the same way for at least 7,500 years.

It was much easier to row a boat downstream, carried along by the current, than upstream. For journeys upriver, donkeys were often used to pull the boats. They could also carry goods across land, where no water route existed.

Large amounts of tin and copper were imported to make bronze. Bronze items, such as tools and weapons, were then sold abroad. Other goods sold abroad included textiles, pottery, barley and dates. Grindstones, which every family needed for grinding barley into flour, were imported in vast quantities from the north. At a place now called Yarim Tepe, archaeologists found a building, dating from 4500BCE, in which a single room held several hundred grindstones. This must have been a merchant's warehouse.

There was long-distance trade with another ancient civilization, the Indus people of northern India, who sold precious stones, such as carnelian. Indian carnelian was used in Mesopotamian jewellery and works of art.

HOW DO WE KNOW?

Objects in Mesopotamian sites made of stone or metal, like the silver boat below, must have been made of materials from other lands. This is evidence of long-distance trade. Seals used by Indian merchants have also been found in Mesopotamian cities, proving that people were trading with India. More evidence comes from many thousands of clay tablets, which include records of business agreements and complaints about the failure to deliver promised goods.

SILVER BOAT
The silver model of a boat, found in a royal grave at Ur, tells us two things about Mesopotamian trade. It shows us what ancient boats looked like, and how they were rowed. It is also made of silver, which is not found in Mesopotamia. Look at the map to see where it might have come from.

RIVER JOURNEY
Mesopotamian boats were rowed, using leaf-shaped oars, or punted: pushed along with a pole driven into the river bed. These boats, with both ends curving up to points, are exactly like modern Iraqi river boats. Pictures of boats on seals show that sails were also used for long sea journeys across the Persian Gulf.

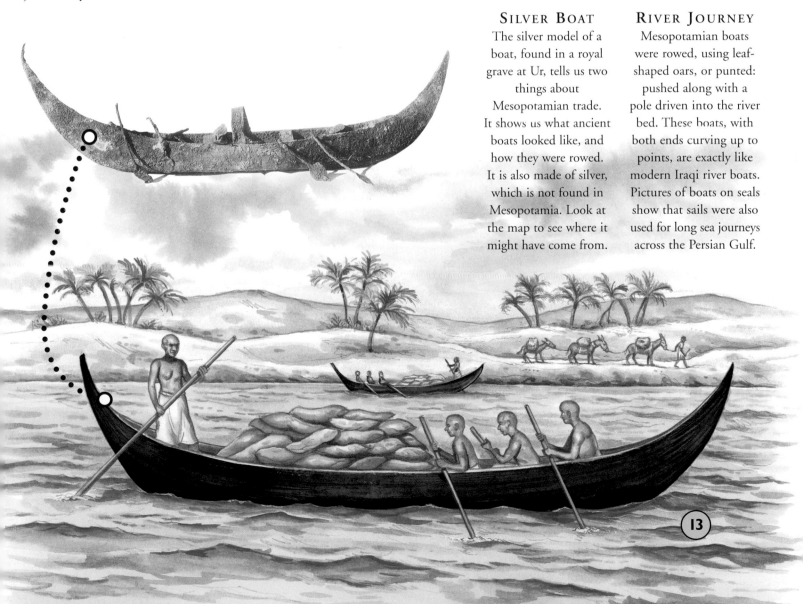

At Home

WEBLINK
http://www.odyssey
adventures.ca/articles/
ur%20of%20the%20
chaldees/ur_article.htm
#houses

Find out all about the
houses of Ur.

Like houses in southern Iraq today, Mesopotamian homes had thick walls of bricks made of mud and chopped straw, dried in the sun. This was the perfect building material to protect the family from the scorching summer heat. Roofs were usually flat, made of palm tree planks with a layer of reed and palm leaf matting, covered with mud.

COURTYARD
A woman grinds barley for making bread in the courtyard of her house. This was hard work, which had to be done every day.

QUERN
Every home had a quern for grinding barley into flour. The upper stone was pushed backwards and forwards over the grain lying in the hollow.

HOW DO WE KNOW?

In the 1920s, many houses in Ur, dating from 1900-1740BCE, were excavated by the British archaeologist Leonard Woolley. Scorched walls and ash-covered floors showed that this part of the city had been destroyed by fire. While the dried mud bricks had mostly crumbled away, the lower parts of walls had survived, for these were made of fired brick. The remains of stairs showed that the houses also had upper floors. From all this Woolley worked out the layout of houses.

COURTYARD HOUSE

Here you can see the courtyard of a house in Ur. We know that this is a courtyard rather than an inside room because it has a paved floor which slopes down towards a central drain, to take away rain water. The walls are very thick, to bear the weight of an upper floor.

For security and privacy, Mesopotamian houses rarely had outside windows. Instead, there was often a courtyard, giving light and air to the rooms of the house. Another reason for this arrangement is given by a tablet, which says, 'rooms opening out of each other are unlucky, but those opening on to a court bring good luck.' The richest people had a central courtyard, with rooms arranged on all four sides, while poorer people might have rooms on just two or three sides, or no courtyard at all. Many of the houses had lavatories, which had paved floors with a hole leading through a pottery drain to a sewer.

A variety of household items have been found, which help us build up a picture of daily life. These include pottery jars, for storing beer and date wine; copper cooking pots; and bowls, plates and cups, made from pottery, stone or copper. Meals were cooked over a fire in the courtyard or in a kitchen. There were also dome-shaped brick ovens, for baking bread.

Tablets from Babylon contain recipes, such as this one for cooking wild hens: 'Assemble the following ingredients in a pot with water: a piece of fat … a carefully measured amount of vinegar … pieces of aromatic wood soaked in beer, and rue leaves. When it comes to the boil, add *samidu* (a spicy plant), leek and garlic mashed with onion. Put the birds in this broth and cook.'

Temples

GIFTS FOR A GOD

These worshippers are bringing gifts for their god, which they present to the priests at the entrance to the temple. Gifts include animals and statuettes of worshippers.

Every Mesopotamian city was believed to belong to a main god or goddess, who was worshipped in a great temple in the centre of the city. The temple was the home of the god, whose statue was kept there.

As well as being the owner of the city, people believed that each god watched over an aspect of life or nature. Nanna, worshipped in Ur, was the moon god. There were also many lesser gods, who oversaw every possible activity, from brick making to brewing beer.

ZIGGURAT

From about 2200BCE, tall stepped towers, called ziggurats, were built at the centre of each temple. This is the ziggurat of Untash, built between 1265-46BCE by King Untash-Gal of Elam. Like all surviving ziggurats, this one has lost its top. Only three of its five levels still stand.

WEBLINK
http://www.crystalinks.
com/ziggurat.html

Find out what we know
about ziggurats and
how they might have
been used.

The people of the city visited the temple to ask their gods favours, or to thank them for granting them. They brought with them gifts, such as animals to be sacrificed (killed as offerings to the god). At Ur, merchants returning from long river journeys would present Nanna with a little silver boat, to thank him for protecting them on their journey.

There was a large staff of priests, priestesses and servants who looked after the god's needs. Twice a day, in the morning and evening, the god was given a meal, which was spread on a table before the statue. On special occasions, the statue was taken out of the temple and carried in a procession through the streets. It was sometimes taken to other cities, so that the god could meet other gods. In wartime, the statues accompanied armies into battle. This gave the soldiers the sense that their god was fighting alongside them.

WEBLINK
http://www.
mesopotamia.co.uk/
gods/challenge/
cha_set.html

Take a challenge to
match the gods with
their cities.

WORSHIPPER
This statuette of a worshipper, his hands clasped in prayer, was presented to the temple of Ninni-Zaza, god of the city of Mari. The statue was supposed to pray to Ninni-Zaza on behalf of the worshipper who presented it. Many statues like this were placed on benches around the inside walls of the temple.

HOW DO WE KNOW?

Around twenty-five ziggurats have been found, some no more than earth mounds. Ancient descriptions help us work out what they looked like. In the fifth century BCE, the Greek writer, Herodotus, visited Babylon and climbed the ziggurat. He said that it had eight levels, with a shelter halfway up, so that people could rest during the climb. On top there was a shrine, in which a bed stood. The Babylonian priests told Herodotus that this was where their god, Bel, slept every night, though Herodotus added, 'I do not believe them'.

There are different ideas about why ziggurats came to be built. Building a tall tower was a way for people on earth to reach up to the heavens, to be closer to the gods who were thought to live there. A ziggurat might also have been meant to represent a sacred mountain, or to be a ladder for the god to climb up to heaven at night.

In the flat Mesopotamian landscape, ziggurats could be seen for miles around, showing the importance of the gods who lived in them, and the wealth and power of the city which had built them.

Kings

KING

This is how the palace of Ur may have looked in about 2500BCE.
The king, sitting on his throne, is served wine made from dates.
The court is entertained by a female singer and a musician playing a plucked stringed instrument, called a lyre.

While each Sumerian city was thought to belong to a god, it was ruled on the god's behalf by a king. According to Sumerian beliefs, the idea of kingship had come down to earth from heaven at the beginning of time. The king was a chief priest, whose main role was to serve the gods. He built and repaired the city's temples, and played a leading role in religious ceremonies, meant to ensure good harvests. He was also a judge, overseeing law and order, and a war leader, who led his city's army into battle. These roles, of

FEAST
This is the peace side of the 'Standard of Ur', which was perhaps the sounding box of a musical instrument. The figures are made from tiny pieces of shell and red sandstone, while the background is lapis lazuli, a blue stone found in what is now Afghanistan.

HOW DO WE KNOW?

Sumerian kings wanted people to remember their achievements. So they had their names stamped on the bricks of the temples they built, and they set up inscriptions recording their victories in war. Lists of kings were also preserved, which help us to work out the sequence of rulers in different cities. Evidence of the daily life of courts comes from goods buried in royal graves, including jewellery, lyres, and the 'Standard of Ur'.

WEBLINK
http://www.wsu.edu:8080/~dee/MESO/GILG.HTM

Find out about Gilgamesh, king of Uruk, the hero of the world's oldest surviving story.

judge and warrior, were also religious. Like kingship, the laws were believed to have come from the gods, and wars were seen as quarrels between rival city gods.

There were a number of different royal titles. A king of a single city was called the *ensi*, which is thought to mean 'lord'. Through warfare, some kings were able to extend their rule over a number of cities. Their title was *lugal*, which means 'big man'.

The beautiful box above was discovered in the 1920s by the British archaeologist, Leonard Woolley, in a royal grave at Ur. Unsure of its purpose, Woolley called it the 'Standard of Ur'. The box has two sides, showing the activities of a king in peace and in war. The peace side depicts a royal feast in the top row. At the top right, you can see a musician playing a lyre and a woman singing. The king, on the left, wears no special royal regalia, such as a crown. However, he can be recognized because he is much bigger than the other figures.

The Great Death Pit

DEATH PIT
One corner of the Death Pit may have looked this just before the earth was piled on top. The women were all found lying on their sides in neat rows, with their legs slightly bent as if they were asleep. Beside each of them was a bowl made of stone or metal.

In 1928-9, the British archaeologist, Leonard Woolley made an amazing discovery while digging in the ancient city of Ur. He found a deep rectangular pit, dating from about 2700-2400BCE, in which sixty-eight women lay buried. By the entrance to the pit, approached by a ramp, six men's bodies lay in a line, as if on guard. This mass grave also contained four lyres and two beautiful statuettes of male goats. Woolley called his discovery 'the Great Death Pit'. Like a detective, he tried to solve the mystery of the burial. How had they died, and why had they been buried with such beautiful treasures?

LYRE
This is one of four lyres discovered in the pit. It was made of wood completely covered in silver, and was decorated with a silver cow's head with eyes of lapis lazuli and shell. Although the wood had rotted away, the silver covering allowed the lyre to be restored.

Woolley had already uncovered many Mesopotamian graves, and was used to finding goods buried with the dead. In most cases, bodies were wrapped in a reed mat and placed in the earth with pots, beads and tools. This was evidence that people believed in a life after death, a next world where they could take their belongings with them. From writings, we know that they called this world 'the land of no return'.

The Death Pit was one of sixteen graves in Ur in which groups of people had been buried with rich treasures, including the 'Standard of Ur', shown on pages 19 and 22. Woolley believed that these were royal graves, and that the people were attendants or courtiers, who had been chosen to accompany their king or queen to the next world.

Because there were no obvious signs of violence, Woolley suggested that the men and women had entered it of their own free will. They had then drunk poison or a sleeping drug from the bowls which lay beside them, before the earth was piled on top.

GOLDEN GOAT

In one corner of the pit, Woolley found this statuette of a male goat. It stands on its hind legs, reaching up to eat the golden leaves of a tree. Its legs and face are covered in gold, while its fleece is made from lapis lazuli and shell. Like the lyre, it was carefully restored after it was discovered.

WEBLINK

http://www. mesopotamia.co.uk/ tombs/explore/exp_ main.html#plan_top

Explore for yourself the tombs Woolley found at Ur.

HOW DO WE KNOW?

Although Woolley's theory explains what might have happened, we will never know for certain if it is true. The bodies were too badly decayed to tell how or when they died. Other theories have been suggested. One idea is that the women were priestesses, who were sacrificed as offerings to the gods. Another is that they were people who were already dead, and whose bodies had been stored elsewhere in order to be finally buried beside their king or queen. The mystery of the Great Death Pit remains.

Warfare

In Sumer, there were a dozen separate city states, which often quarrelled with each other over farm land or the water supply. These quarrels often led to warfare. Each of the cities was surrounded by a strong brick wall, needed for protection from other cities and also foreign invaders.

The first recorded war took place in about 2500BCE, between the cities of Lagash and Umma. Eannatum, king of Lagash, won the war and then had a stele, or upright stone, set up, celebrating his victory. It shows his army on the march, while his dead enemies are being eaten by vultures. Another victorious Sumerian army, from about the same time, is shown below, on the 'Standard of Ur'.

In an inscription of about 2050BCE, Shulgi, king of Ur, boasted of his skill at winning battles, which he claimed to fight on behalf of his god, Enlil: 'When I set off for battle to a place that Enlil has commanded me, I go ahead of my troops. I have a passion for weapons. Not only do I carry my spear and lance, I also know how to handle a sling. The clay pellets that I shoot fly around like a violent rainstorm. In my rage I do not let them miss.'

WEBLINK
http://joseph_berrigan.
tripod.com/ancient
babylon/id46.html

Find out about warfare among the early Sumerians.

STANDARD OF UR
The war side of the Standard of Ur (see page 19) shows four-wheeled chariots, pulled by onagers (wild asses), and soldiers armed with spears and axes. In the top row, soldiers bring prisoners to the king, who has just stepped down from his chariot.

22

INTO BATTLE

Sumerian soldiers marched in tight ranks, protected by long shields, probably made of leather on wooden frames. They carried bronze pointed spears and wore copper helmets. The king and his leading men rode chariots into battle.

We can also read laments, poems of sorrow, which show us the viewpoint of the defeated. This lament was written after Ur was destroyed by the Elamites, in 2000BCE: 'Ur is destroyed, bitter is its lament. The country's blood now fills its holes like hot bronze in a mould... Our temple is destroyed, the gods have abandoned us...'

HOW DO WE KNOW?

As well as the victory stele (see page 22) and the 'Standard of Ur', archaeologists have found much evidence for early Mesopotamian warfare. The soldiers buried in the Death Pit at Ur wore copper helmets, just like those shown on the standard. Weapons including bronze axes, spears and swords have also been discovered. Digging at Ur, Leonard Woolley found that large areas of the city were blackened by fire, evidence of Ur's second destruction, by the Babylonians, in 1738BCE.

The King's Laws

RIVER TRIAL
This woman is being thrown into the River Euphrates, as a trial by ordeal, a type of test. If she survives, she will be declared innocent and freed. If she drowns, it will be a sign that the gods have judged her guilty and punished her. King Hammurabi watches from the river bank.

24

KING AND GOD
On top of the stele of Hammurabi is a carving of the king standing before Shamash, god of justice and the sun, identified by flames rising from his shoulders. The picture was meant to show that the king was making laws on behalf of the god of justice.

One of the most important duties of a Mesopotamian king was to oversee justice. Kings had to give decisions in quarrels over land or property, and they tried and punished criminals. They also wrote the first laws, in which they listed punishments for various crimes, and described how cases should be judged. The most complete early law list is that of King Hammurabi, ruler of Babylon from 1792-50BCE. He had his laws carved on a 2.25-metre high cone-shaped stone stele.

Hammurabi's stele has forty-nine columns in which 282 laws are listed. Among them, a son who struck his father would have both his hands chopped off. A man who put out the eye of another man would have his own eye put out. Most of these laws were not invented by Hammurabi, but were based on existing customs. The stele describes a 'river ordeal', shown in the picture on the left, used when it was not clear if someone accused of a serious crime was guilty or innocent. This ordeal is also described in the oldest known law code, written three hundred years before Hammurabi's time, by a king of Ur.

At the end of the list, Hammurabi explained that he had set the stele up as an example to later rulers: 'To the end of days, forever, may the king who happens to be in the land observe the words of justice which I have inscribed on my stele… let that stele reveal to him the accustomed way, the way to follow, the land's judgements which I have judged.'

WEBLINK
http://eawc.evansville.edu/anthology/hammurabi.htm

Read all the laws of Hammurabi.

HOW DO WE KNOW?
The stele of Hammurabi was discovered in the winter of 1901, by the French archaeologist, Jean-Vincent Scheil. He found it not in Babylon, where Hammurabi had set it up, but in Susa, capital of Elam, in present-day Iran. In 1165BCE, the Elamites attacked Babylon and took the stele away with them as booty. When Scheil found the stele, it was broken into three pieces. He put them back together, and then spent six months translating the writing. Today, you can see Hammurabi's stele in the Louvre Museum in Paris.

Empire

The most warlike Mesopotamian people were the Assyrians, who lived in the northern cities of Ashur, Ninevah, Nimrud and Khorsabad. Between 950 and 612BCE, the Assyrians conquered an empire which stretched across the Middle East, from western Persia (now Iran) to northern Egypt.

The wealth of the Assyrian Empire allowed kings to build some of the biggest palaces found in Mesopotamia. Palace walls were covered in painted stone reliefs showing kings worshipping gods, hunting lions, and leading the Assyrian army into battle. The aim was to impress any visitor to the palace with the power of the Assyrian king.

WINGED BULL
This great winged bull with a human head stood guard by a doorway in the palace of King Sargon II in Khorsabad. Similar winged bulls and lions have been found in several Assyrian palaces.

SARGON
King Sargon II, who ruled the Assyrian Empire from 721-705BCE, leads a procession through his vast palace at Khorsabad.

WEBLINK

http://www.mesopotamia.
co.uk/palaces
/home_set.html

http://www.mesopotamia.
co.uk/warfare/
index.html

Find out about the
palaces of Assyria and
Assyrian warfare.

ATTACK
This wall carving of
Assyrian soldiers
attacking a city was
found in the palace of
King Tiglath-piliser III
in Nimrud. At the
bottom, enemy heads
are chopped off. In one
palace inscription, an
Assyrian king boasted,
'I cut off their heads
and piled them up at
the walls of their cities
like heaps of grain.'

By the first millennium BCE, many new ways of fighting had
been invented. Bronze weapons had been replaced by iron
ones, which were harder and sharper-edged. The Assyrians
also used horses, which they rode and used to pull fast two-
wheeled chariots. They were expert at capturing walled cities,
using great battering rams and siege towers. They were also
extremely cruel. Wall carvings in Assyrian palaces show
defeated enemies being skinned alive, while palace
inscriptions left by kings boast of their cruelty: 'I built a pillar
over against his city gate and I skinned all the chief men …
and I covered the pillar with their skins. Some I walled up
within the pillar, some I impaled upon the pillar on stakes.'

HOW DO WE KNOW?

Unlike earlier Mesopotamian peoples, such as the Sumerians,
the Assyrians were never forgotten. The Bible describes their
destruction of the kingdom of Israel, when they carried off
ten Jewish tribes, who were never heard from again. Between
CE1842-55, an Englishman, Austen Henry Layard, and a
Frenchman, Paul-Emile Botta, rediscovered the Assyrian cities,
in what is now northern Iraq. They uncovered palace wall
carvings, showing the army on campaign, and found Assyrian
accounts which backed up the Bible story of the destruction
of Israel.

Eventually, the cruelty of
the Assyrians led to
widespread rebellions. The
king of Babylon joined
forces with people called
the Medes, (who lived to
the east of Mesopotamia),
and destroyed the empire.
In 614-612BCE, the Assyrian
cities were burned to the
ground.

Timeline

c. 5000BCE Farmers from northern Mesopotamia move into the flat southern plains.

c. 4000-3500BCE Villages at Ur, Uruk and other southern sites grow into towns.

c. 3500-2800BCE The towns grow into cities. Large temples are built.

c. 3100BCE Earliest known use of cuneiform writing, in Uruk.

c. 3000BCE Bronze used for tools and weapons. Four-wheeled chariot used in war.

c. 2750-2400BCE First dynasty of Ur. Kings and queens of Ur are buried in rich mass graves.

c. 2500BCE Earliest recorded war, between Lagash and Umma.

c. 2330BCE Sargon of Akkad conquers all of Sumer.

c. 2220BCE The Gutians from Gutium in the eastern mountains conquer Akkad and Sumer.

c. 2113-2096BCE Reign of Ur-Nammu, founder of the third dynasty of Ur, who throws off Gutian rule.

c. 2095-47BCE Reign of Shulgi of Ur, who builds the great ziggurat.

c. 2000BCE The Elamites (from Elam in the east) destroy Ur and capture the king.

c. 1900BCE The Amorites (people from the western deserts) conquer much of Mesopotamia, ruling from Babylon.

1792-50BCE Reign of King Hammurabi of Babylon, who rules over Akkad and Sumer, now called Babylonia, and part of Assyria.

1738BCE Ur destroyed again, by the Babylonians.

c. 1600BCE Two foreign peoples, the Hittites and Kassites, invade Mesopotamia.

Iron weapons and fast chariots pulled by horses now used in war.

c. 1570BCE Kassite kings rule Babylon. Their dynasty rules for almost 500 years.

c. 950BCE Assyrians begin to conquer their empire.

612BCE Fall of the Assyrian Empire, replaced by the Babylonian Empire.

605-562BCE Reign of Nebuchadrezzar II of Babylon, who conquers Syria and Palestine, destroys Jerusalem and takes the Jews as captives to Babylon.

539BCE Cyrus the Great of Persia conquers Babylonian Empire.

331BCE Alexander the Great of Macedon (to the north of Ancient Greece) conquers the Persian Empire. He makes Babylon his capital.

c. CE75 Last use of cuneiform script.

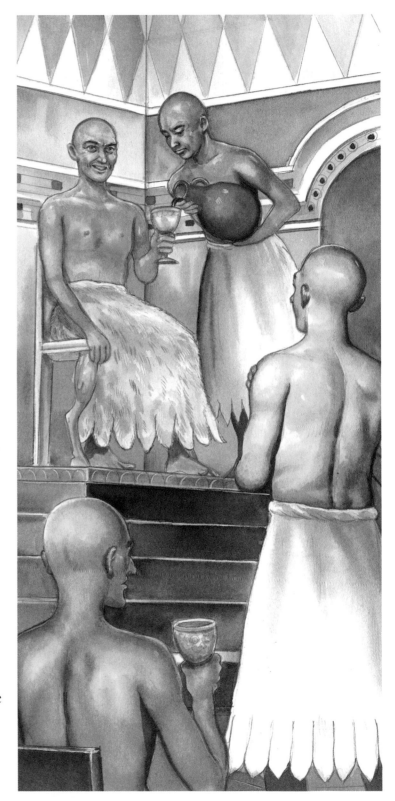

Glossary

Akkad Central region of Mesopotamia, where the Tigris and Euphrates come closest together.

Akkadian The name given to the people from Akkad, and also the language spoken in Akkad.

Archaeologist A person who finds out about the past by looking for the remains of buildings and other objects, often beneath the ground.

Assyria Northern region of Mesopotamia, based on the cities of Ashur, Ninevah, Nimrud and Khorsabad.

Babylonia The name given to Sumer and Akkad after they were united under the rule of the kings of Babylon.

BCE Used in dates. Means 'before the Common Era'.

Bitumen Natural tar, which seeps out of the ground.

Carnelian Precious red stone found in India, also spelled 'cornelian'.

CE Used in dates. Means 'the Common Era'. The common Era begins with year 1 which is the same as the year AD1 in the Christian calendar.

Cuneiform Writing system used in Mesopotamia. The name means 'wedge shaped'.

Cylinder seal A roller-shaped piece of stone, shell or metal, carved with pictures and writing, pressed into clay or wax to sign letters and seal containers or doors.

Date A sweet, dark brown, oval fruit which grows on a tall palm tree.

Dynasty A family line of kings

Elam Country to the east of Sumer, with a capital at Susa, in present-day Iran.

Elamite The name given to the people from Elam, and also the language spoken in Elam.

Fertile crescent Semi-circular region stretching from the Mediterranean to the Persian Gulf, where farming was first practised. 'Fertile' means able to produce new life.

Indus Civilization Early Indian civilization, lasting from 3100-1700 BC, based on cities around the River Indus in northern India.

Irrigation The control of water for the purposes of farming. An example is the digging of a canal or ditch, to take water from a river to a field.

Lapis lazuli A bright blue stone used in jewellery and sculptures.

Mesopotamia The Greek name for the land between the Tigris and the Euphrates rivers. It means 'between the rivers'.

Onager A wild ass.

Persia The region to the east of Mesopotamia, now called Iran.

Pollination To sprinkle pollen on a flower, so that it can produce fruit.

Reservoir A specially built place for storing water.

Sacrifice Killing an animal as an offering to a god.

Scribe A person who writes or keeps records.

Further information

Sewer An underground pipe or channel for carrying away waste and water.

Shrine A building housing something holy, such as the statue of a god.

Siege When an army surrounds a town or a building and cuts off its supplies, to force the people inside to surrender.

Silt Fine soil carried by water.

Stele Upright stone or pillar carved with an inscription or picture, usually on behalf of a ruler.

Stylus Pointed instrument, such as a cut reed, used for writing on clay or wax.

Sumer The southern region of Mesopotamia, where the first cities such as Ur and Uruk were built.

Sumerian The name given to the people from Sumer, and also the language spoken in Sumer.

Tablet A small flat piece of clay, used for writing on.

Tell An Arabic word for a mound. Tells are made of fallen walls, pottery, stones and other rubbish left behind by ancient settlements.

Ziggurat A tall temple tower resembling a pyramid, but built in stepped stages with a shrine on top.

BOOKS

The City of Rainbows: A Tale from Ancient Sumer by Karen Foster (University of Pennsylvania Museum Publications, 1999)

Find out about Mesopotamia: What Life Was Like in Ancient Sumer, Babylon and Assyria by Lorna Oakes (Southwater, 2003)

First Civilisations (Cultural Atlas for Young People) by Erica C D Hunter, (Facts on File Ltd, 1994)

First Civilisations: From 10,000BC to 1500BC by Anne Millard (Usborne Publishing Ltd, 1992)

Looking Back: Mesopotamia and the Near East: From 10,000BC to 539BC by John Malam (Evans Brothers, 1999)

CD-ROM

Atlas of the Ancient World (Maris Multimedia Ltd, 1997)

Index